ARISTOTLE

ON THE

ART OF POETRY

ARISTOTLE

ON THE

ART OF POETRY

A LECTURE WITH TWO APPENDICES

BY

A. O. PRICKARD, M.A.,

FELLOW OF NEW COLLEGE, OXFORD

" Homo qui erranti comiter monstrat viam
Quasi lumen de suo lumine accendat facit ;
Nihilominus ipsi lucet, quum illi accenderit."—ENNIUS.

London

MACMILLAN AND CO.

AND NEW YORK

1891

PREFATORY NOTE

THIS lecture was prepared in compliance
with an invitation from the Alexandrian
and Philosophical Clubs of the University
of Glasgow, which reached me through
my friend Professor Ramsay ; and was
read to them (with some omissions) on
12th December 1890. It is printed,
partly because the writer has from time
to time been engaged upon the *Poetics*
in the ordinary course of Oxford work,
and is glad of an opportunity of giving
a more general treatment to some of its
points, partly in the hope that where he

is at fault in fact or inference he may be corrected by some who are more familiar with Aristotle. He has attempted to give a plain account of the chief judgments passed by a very clear thinker upon the considerable body of poetical literature accessible to him ; and also to indicate some among them which seem to be, in pre - eminent degree, of lasting value and application. In Appendix A are added references to passages from Greek and Latin authors, and notes on one or two questions which called for more detailed examination. In Appendix B is a list, doubtless incomplete, of the principal editions of and commentaries upon the *Poetics*. The great literary merit of the edition of Twining, and the penetrating scholarship of that of Tyrwhitt, call for a special recognition.

The numerical references in the text of the lecture are to notes in Appendix A ; the marginal references are to chapters of the *Poetics*.

Aristotle Knew.
Yes and Homer could unwind
A spool of experience
But what of this other thought?
These words of sorrow scribbled
on the back of my soul.
Ellen never loved me.

Herne Relft

ARISTOTLE ON THE ART
OF POETRY

Felix qui potuit rerum cognoscere causas—

Fortunatus et ille, deos qui novit agrestes.

THE short treatise on the Art of Poetry
known to us as the *Poetics*[1] comes
into our hands recommended, even before
we open the volume, by several different
considerations. It is the work of no ordinary man of letters (though Aristotle
was a lover of books, and perhaps the first
who ever formed a library), but of a man
who might have said of himself, as only
one or two could say in the history of our
race, that he had "taken all knowledge
for his province"; who, while dealing[2]

with the problems of the physical world, and with those of abstract and applied thought, and with the conditions of human nature, in the individual and in the body-politic, found his survey incomplete unless it included those Arts which ensure to us the gifts of ordered and beautiful speech— Rhetoric and her sister Poetry. Again, this is the earliest attempt to treat deliberately, and in set form, the subject of literature. The ground had been prepared by the teaching of the rhetoricians, by the Middle Comedy, above all by the speculations of Plato, so lofty and so penetrating, yet often ironical and sometimes bewildering ; but here for the first time questions as to the nature and office of Poetry are asked directly and are answered with authority. And, once more, over what a noble field of existing poetry did the gaze of the philosopher travel : Homer, the whole of Greek Tragedy,—for in Aristotle's time Tragedy, for all creative purposes, was a thing of the past,[3]——the whole of the Old Comedy, the whole of Greek Lyric. The poetry of the world, as we now know it, is doubtless a fuller as well as a more complex whole than this. Many languages, new civilisations, intellectual forces unknown to the Greek, a widening of the affections [4] inconceivable to the ancient world, have renovated and enriched the material which is still poured into poetic moulds. Yet something is gained to the critic whose effort is concentrated on a single language ; and what single volume of national poetry can compare in brilliance with that which was open to Aristotle——what in life and in life-giving power ? And, lastly, how much of the literary criticism of later time has been avowedly based on the results obtained by him. Often his words have been misunderstood, and his authority claimed for doctrines which he never contemplated. Yet how many has his method impelled to true inquiry ; how often has he been a guide to reasonable and fruitful judgments ; how many of his conclusions, faithfully worked out in the field of his own observation, remain literally true for the wider regions in which the modern critic moves.

I ask you to-day, first, to look into the substance and content of the *Poetics*, in the form in which the book has come down to us ; and afterwards to examine some of the leading thoughts which are, as you will see, successively brought under our notice in it.

In approaching the book itself two cautions are not unnecessary. First, let us not be disappointed if we fail to find much which we may have expected to be there. The treatment (let us at once allow it) is severe and scientific ; there is not a very large addition to our knowledge of facts about Greek poetry ; there are few judgments about particular poets and their works. And, secondly, let us be content with what is written, not asking to read into the words of the Greek writer our own thoughts, formed among surroundings and traditions other than his, and, in some points, essentially different.

We will now take the opening sentence, and consider the plan of treatment which the Author, with care and close definition, proposes to himself.

"My design is to treat of Poetry in C. 1. general and of its several species—to inquire, what is the proper effect of each —what construction of a fable or plan is essential to a good Poem—of what and how many parts each species consists; with whatever else belongs to the same subject: and I shall begin, as Nature directs, with first principles." [5]

The several species of poetry here mentioned are explained to be Tragedy, Epic, Comedy, and Lyric; the other matters belonging to the same inquiry

are those connected with the other Fine
Arts, and especially with Music and
Dancing, or Pantomime : the first principle, which is enunciated in the next
sentence, is that of Imitation.

How is this undertaking fulfilled in the
book before us ? Partially, it must be
answered, and too shortly. Of one of
the species, Tragedy, we have a full examination. There is a carefully drawn
definition of Tragedy, which tells us what
it is and what it does ; it is analysed into
six constituent parts or elements, which
are considered in order ; and practical
rules are laid down for the management
of Plot, to which special prominence
had been already given in the opening
sentence. Yet even here we shall see
that there are gaps in important parts of
the argument ; as is clear, not only to the
sense of the reader, but also from the
terms in which the Author refers to the
Poetics in his other works ; there some-

times seems to have been misplacement of material; on the other hand some chapters have appeared to scholars to be the work of a later hand, of a grammarian rather than a philosopher. Epic poetry is treated far more shortly, yet perhaps not inadequately, when it is remembered that Aristotle considered Tragedy to have in a sense superseded Epic, as the more complex and manifold organism supersedes that which is simpler; so that the results obtained for Tragedy are up to a certain point capable of being transferred to Epic; and the inquiry need not begin over again, or be conducted independently. The notice of Comedy is extremely slight; of Lyric there is hardly a word. About Poetry itself, the whole Art as contrasted with its own species, there is little except what arises incidentally in the discussion of Tragedy. One chapter, indeed, of great interest and value, traces the Art from its earliest beginnings, and its

development under its several heads, until
its full and final proportions were reached
in the forms of Tragedy and Comedy.
But we have no definition of the nature
and office of Poetry; little about poets
and their claims upon our hearing.

After making allowance for the supreme
importance attached to Tragedy, and the
probability that the treatment of the other
species would be slighter, and that Poetry
itself would be approached through Tragedy
and not independently, we cannot fail to
conclude that the work as we have it is
fragmentary.   And, in fact, external evidence bears out this presumption.   In the
lists of Aristotle's works framed in the
second century A.D.[6] we find mention made
of a work entitled *Enquiry into Poetic Art*
in two books, of another *Concerning Poets*
in three books; another is called *Didas-
caliæ*, another *Difficulties in Homer*.   It
seems reasonable to suppose that the first
of these works is represented to us by the

Poetics : the existence of the others, now lost, not only testifies to the interest taken by Aristotle in literature and its problems, but also explains why we ought not to look for much statement of facts in the extant book. Just as Bacon placed his *Historia Naturalis* before his theoretic work ; just as Aristotle himself collected accounts of the constitutions of a hundred and fifty-eight states before he wrote the *Politics* ; so in the case of Poetry the book *Concerning Poets* and the others contained the historical material : that which is in part preserved to us embodies his philosophical judgments upon the facts so brought together.

Happily, in spite of such gaps as I have indicated, and although we do not know how the work was put into its present form, the general argument is clear and satisfactory. I take up the account of its contents from the opening sentence. The general principle that all Poetry rests on C. I.

Imitation having been laid down, the various kinds of Poetry, with the arts most nearly akin to it, are next compared with one another in respect of this principle. This is done under three heads, treated in three successive chapters ; the instruments or means of the imitation, its object, and its manner being taken separately. The process of comparison may appear some-what mechanical ; it is supplemented by C. 4. the historical chapter, to which I have already referred, one very weighty and luminous, and by one on the special history of Comedy ; and the results are then stated C. 6. for Tragedy in the famous Definition :—

" Tragedy is an imitation of some action that is important, entire, and of a proper magnitude, by language embellished and rendered pleasurable—the different kinds of embellishment being kept sepa-rate in the different parts—in the way, not of narrative, but of action ; effecting through Pity and Terror the purgation of such passions or tendencies." An explanation follows :—" By pleasurable language I mean a language that has the embellishments of rhythm, melody, and metre. And I add ' by different means in different parts,' because in some parts metre alone is employed, in others melody."

You will observe that this Definition is in two parts. In the first we are told what Tragedy *is*, in the second what it *does*.[7] The first part states the " genus " and " differentia" of Tragedy : by genus it is, according to the first principle laid down on the first page, a form of Imitation ; the differentia is stated in the clauses which gather up the results of the first three chapters, and contrast Tragedy successively with the various kindred arts, under the three heads of comparison already mentioned. The second part states the effect or office of Tragedy ; namely, to work upon the feelings of Pity and Fear in a particular manner, which has not so far been explained, and which in fact is not explained in any part of the *Poetics*. The first part takes its significance from the word *Mimesis*, or Imitation ; the second from the word *Katharsis*, or Purgation. It is not too much to say that in these two words, rightly understood, lies the whole of Aristotle's teaching on Tragedy, so far, at least, as it is theoretical. We will return to them presently for a more particular examination.

C. 6. The inquiry starts afresh from this point, and the six constituent "parts" of Tragedy are determined. This is done by a process something like chemical analysis ; or, if we may vary the figure, like that by which the sections of the cone are derived from the solid figure, viewed under different aspects. On the first view of Tragedy you see that it is a performance given before the eyes of spectators : therefore *Spectacle* (in which term is included all that meets the eye—scenery, grouping

of persons on the stage, and the like) is
its most obvious element. Ask next by
what means these performers effect their
imitation, and you find that they use
words and music : therefore *musical composition* and *verbal diction* are also elements
of Tragedy. Ask further what it is which
these performers seek thus to imitate, and
the answer is that they reproduce the
actions of men, or men engaged in action ;
men who have each a moral character, and
each an intellectual habit or faculty, which
are the two determinants of all that is
done or said. Hence the poet must reproduce *Character* and *Thought* (convention-
ally translated Sentiment), and he must
further and above all reproduce the story
or *Plot*, which is in fact the action itself ;
and these are three additional parts, or
elements, of Tragedy. The six parts must
be present in all Tragedy, though the rela-
tive importance attached to each may vary
with different poets, and in different plays.

But the order of derivation is not the order of intrinsic worth. Plot stands far above the rest ; and for this judgment, which is highly characteristic of Aristotle, but which must not be accepted without reserve, a series of reasons is given. Character is second, since men are only less interesting than men's actions. Thought and Language follow. Music and Spectacle are dismissed ; because, though of great practical importance, they have little to do with the Art of Poetry considered apart from that which is subsidiary to it, and they do not concern the critic or theorist. The other four are treated in order. In connection with Plot the following questions are discussed — How long should a play be? What standard of Unity is required? Must the incidents be true in the same sense as the facts of the historian ? What is the place, to use a modern phrase, of "poetical justice"? At this point, Plot is itself analysed into

C. 7.

C. 8.

C. 9.

C. 10.

four constituents : Peripeteia (or Evolution) and Recognition, which together are the distinguishing signs of a complex plot ; Character, and Suffering, which, if unsupported by the other two, belong to the simple plot. This second analysis, valuable as it is, may be found confusing, the more so as Character figures twice over, once as an independent part of Tragedy, once as a part of Plot. The actions which may possibly be treated in a tragedy are then considered with special reference to their power of working upon Pity and Fear. Recognition receives a very full C. 16. examination, cases found in actual plays being considered and classified.

Under the head of Character four points are noted. The characters must be *good*, C. 15. that is, must not fall below a certain level of worthiness and elevation ; they must be *suitable* to conditions of age, sex, or station, *like* the characters found in Nature or in literature, and lastly *uniform* ; and again

illustrations are given from Greek plays.
It is interesting to notice in passing that
Aristotle's four rules for Character, or at
any rate three of them, will be found
in the *Ars Poetica* of Horace, a work
perhaps deriving much of its detail,
though not directly, from the *Poetics*;
and certainly written from an assured
conviction that a Roman poet, writing for
a grave Roman public, must above all
things study Character.[8]

The third element of Tragedy, Thought,
is only treated by reference to the
Rhetoric. For the stage speaker and the
speaker of real life must draw upon the
same faculty, to ensure that what they say
shall be adapted to the circumstances
under which they speak. Thus Ajax
about to fall upon his sword, or Clytemnestra exulting over her accomplished
deed of blood, go to the same storehouse
of thought as a real speaker in a great
crisis of affairs; and what Ajax or

Clytemnestra says the poet must conceive ;
so that the faculty of thought which he
appears to copy is in fact part of his
own equipment.

The fourth element, Diction, is also CC. 19-22.
common to Rhetoric, but is treated independently.   The various deviations from
plain or literal speech which may make
words and expressions poetical are carefully explained; the treatment of Metaphor,
both simple and compound, being especially lucid.

The account of Tragedy is now com- CC. 23, 24.
plete, and we pass to Epic Poetry, to
which the results obtained for Tragedy
are, so far as the conditions admit, applied.
For Tragedy is, as we saw, the more complex organism, and of its six parts two
(Music and Spectacle) have no place in
Epic.   Some interesting criticism of the
Iliad and *Odyssey*, and of other so-called
Homeric poems, is given ; but the treatment is intentionally slight.   A long and C. 25.

C

difficult chapter follows, in which difficulties currently alleged against poets,
especially Homer, are stated, and methods
C. 26. of solution offered.   In the last chapter
of the book Epic Poetry and Tragedy
are compared in point of excellence, and
the palm is, on the whole, awarded to
Tragedy.

It will be seen that the treatise is far
fuller on Tragedy than on any of the
other branches of Poetry ; also that it is
partly speculative, where the phenomena
of poetry are examined, and its nature
and office determined ; in part critical,
embodying rules for writing a good
play, and for judging those which are
already in our hands.   Let us look first
at Aristotle's theory of Tragedy, in which
much of his theory of Poetry is involved.

C. 6.   " All Tragedy is a *Mimesis*, and it
effects a *Katharsis*."   We will take the
two terms in order.

In a certain superficial sense it is at

once plain that dramatic poetry is imitative, because it copies, or mimics, the doings of men. In another sense, also superficial, we can understand how some descriptive poetry is called imitative, the word being here borrowed from the art of Painting. But that neither of these will satisfy Aristotle's meaning we shall readily see if we consider the groups into which he arranges the various Fine Arts. Poetry in its several forms, Music in most of its forms, are all imitative arts. To the group thus formed he presently adds Dancing, or Pantomime; which, it need hardly be said, was so practised among the Greeks, and among other Southern European peoples, as to attain the dignity of a Fine Art.[9] Painting and Sculpture are also, no doubt, arts of imitation ; but they belong to another group, and are always mentioned by way of illustration only.[10] Can we then so far attain to Aristotle's point of view as to see how

Poetry, Music, and Dancing cohere, and form a homogeneous group?

You will remember that, after laying down the general principle of Imitation, Aristotle proceeded to consider the different members of this group; taking three points in the imitation—its instruments, its object, and its manner—which he used as so many criteria for distinguishing the several arts, and in particular for comparing Tragedy with each of the others. Let us take the same three points, and ask under each head what the arts of our group have in common with one another, but not with Painting or Sculpture. First, by what means, or instruments, do they all imitate? Aristotle gives the answer: by rhythm, melody, and language; or some one, or some combination of these. Now by what do Painting and Sculpture imitate? Again let him answer: by colours and outlines. Secondly, what is it which our arts have to imitate? The actions, characters, and passions of men. But does not the painter also imitate these? Yes, says Aristotle, in another work,[11] but not immediately. The painter imitates the outward embodiment or sign of the passion, say, of anger, or of the action of an angry man ; the musician or poet imitates the very passion itself. Thirdly, what is the manner, or process, of imitation? The answer to this question is not given by Aristotle, but may be readily supplied. Poetry, Music, and Dancing all suppose performers—one or many, and an audience or body of spectators. Painting and Sculpture work by a permanent representation of the thing intended. So Poetry is, like Music, but unlike Painting, an audible, direct, momentary presentment of the actions and feelings of men.

Again, the unity and common basis of these arts may be seen in another way, if we remember that all were developed out of a single elementary art. The minstrel of early days sang and played, and the performance was helped out by gesticulation or dance.[12]   Song, says Plato,[13] has three elements, rhythm, melody, language—the very same three used by our arts ; which have in fact come into being by the expansion, on different sides, of the simple original performance of the minstrel.

Let us now try to understand what this principle of imitation is which we have seen to be shared by Poetry and Music. C. 4. We will turn to the fourth chapter, where a historical sketch is given of the evolution of Poetry.

Poetry, regarded as a whole, owes its being to two causes, both natural.   First, there is the instinct of imitation — the desire to copy the actions and gestures of others ; which is shared to some extent by the other animals, but is characteristic of man from his cradle.   This it is which sets the infant to delight in his mimic creations ; a picture familiar to us from Wordsworth's lines :

> See, at his feet, some little plan or chart,
> Some fragment from his dream of human life,
> Shaped by himself with newly-learned art ;
> A wedding or a festival,
> A mourning or a funeral ;
> And this hath now his heart,
> And unto this he frames his song :
> Then will he fit his tongue
> To dialogues of business, love, or strife ;
> But it will not be long
> Ere this be thrown aside,
> And with new joy and pride
> The little Actor cons another part ;
> Filling from time to time his "humorous stage"
> With all the Persons, down to palsied Age,
> That Life brings with her in her equipage ;
> As if his whole vocation
> Were endless imitation.

Next, it is also an instinct of man's nature to take pleasure in recognising things imitated by others. Whether Aristotle intended this to be his second natural cause is not quite clear : it may well, perhaps better, be regarded as the obverse or subjective side of the instinct first

mentioned.[14]   In any case, the pleasure
seems to be derived through a process
of the intellect : you look at a picture, or
other work of imitation, and you recognise,
by a sudden flash of thought, that this is
such - and - such a person or landscape.
This gratifies that universal desire of add-
ing to our knowledge which Aristotle,
" Master of those who know," imputes
without reserve to every member of the
human family.[15]   The pleasure is pro-
portionate to the speed and sureness of
the process of thought, just as a word
or metaphor which bears in upon us a
thought more quickly than its prosaic
equivalent, is always a vehicle of delight.[16]
But the desire of imitation, and the pleasure which we take in discerning imitation,
are not all.   There is a further physical
cause special to Poetry, or shared by it
with Music ; and this is what we understand by ear—the charms of melody and
rhythm, and especially of that branch of

rhythm known as metre. Here then are
two factors in our nature, distinct and
independent of one another — first, the
imitative instinct; secondly, the delicate
perceptions of ear : and Poetry is, if we
may borrow a mathematical word, a function or outcome of these two. Let us
watch the process at work. In the earliest
and rudest times there were those who
felt, more than their fellows, an impulse
which stirred them to reproduce, to themselves or to those about them, the feelings
by which they had been moved. But as
they did so, they found that their rude
improvisations took an added charm when
they fell into rhythmical words and movements and sounds. By degrees the
imitation became more refined and subtle,
and association gave fuller shades of
meaning to what at first was mere
mimicry ; while, at the same time, the
other element, that of rhythm and cadence,
was beautified and enlarged ; and at last,

after several such stages were passed, there was no longer a rude extemporaneous utterance, but—a poem.   But the original motive had taken two different directions : some of the early inhabitants of the world whose feelings overflowed thus readily were of the graver sort, others of the lighter.   Hence hymns to gods and panegyrics of heroes on the one hand ; hence rough abuse of a neighbour on the other.   The growth of poetry still went on, and both tendencies met in Homer, the grander exemplified by his *Iliad* and *Odyssey*, the more ignoble in the *Margites*, a curious poem of so-called Homeric authorship, in which mere abuse had made way for that raillery directed at another's weakness or clumsiness which is in essence humorous.   And still poetry grew : Tragedy, with its fuller organism, was the outcome of Epic ; Comedy displaced its simpler predecessors.   And each grew on its own ground ; and in particular, those stories of mythology which were great enough to bear the weight of Tragedy lived down those which were slighter. And now, says Aristotle, though the full resources of Tragedy, in all its branches, may not have been exhausted, and future poets may yet make it stronger in particular directions ; yet the process of natural growth is over, the organism, as we know it, is complete.

In this paraphrase of Aristotle's words I have not read into them anything which is not there ; at least it has been my endeavour not to do so : more likely I have failed to render many particulars in his account, and some qualifications. But the theory itself is so strikingly and beautifully set out by Shelley in his *Defence of Poetry* (whether consciously or by coincidence of idea I do not know [17]), that, at the risk of some repetition, I must ask you to listen to a few of his sentences.

" A child at play by itself will express its delight by its voice and motions ; and

every inflexion of tone and every gesture
will bear exact relation to a corresponding
antitype in the pleasurable impressions
which awakened it ; it will be the reflected
image of that impression ; and as the lyre
trembles and sounds after the wind has
died away, so the child seeks, by prolong-
ing in its voice and motions the duration
of the effect, to prolong also a consciousness of the cause.   In relation to the
objects which delight a child, these expressions are what poetry is to higher
objects.   The savage (for the savage is to
ages what the child is to years) expresses
the emotions produced in him by sur-
rounding objects in a similar manner ;
and language and gesture, together with
plastic or pictorial imitation, become the
image of the combined effects of those
objects, and of his apprehension of them.
Man in society, with all his passions and
his pleasures, next becomes the object of
the passions and pleasures of man ; an

additional class of emotions produce an augmented treasure of expressions ; and language, gesture, and the imitative arts become at once the representation and the medium, the pencil and the picture, the chisel and the statue, the chord and the harmony."

And again :

" In the youth of the world men dance and sing, and imitate natural objects, observing in these actions, as in all others, a certain rhythm or order. And although all men observe a similar, they observe not the same order in the motions of the dance, in the melody of the song, in the combinations of language, in the series of their imitation of natural objects. For there is a certain order or rhythm belonging to each of these classes of mimetic representation, from which the hearer and the spectator receive an intenser and purer pleasure than from any other. The sense of an approximation to this order has been called taste by modern writers."

To recapitulate : in laying the foundation of poetry in imitation, Aristotle asserts the identity of its operation with music ; since in both arts men, obeying an imperious instinct, reproduce, for themselves or for those about them, the feelings which they have themselves experienced. It would seem to follow that, upon this view, taken in its full strictness, lyric poetry should be the most imitative of all the kinds; more imitative than Tragedy, except so far as Tragedy, according to Greek usage, incorporates Lyric with itself. But there is another and more obvious sense of the word, in which the drama, mimicking directly the details of human action, is most imitative ; and the two senses cannot always be kept apart. The distinction is finely laid down by De Quincey in a paper on *The Antigone of Sophocles.* He writes :

" In this argument " (one directed against oratorio or lyrical drama) " lies an ignorance of the very first principle concerned in *every* Fine Art. In all alike, more or less directly, the object is to reproduce in the mind some great effect, through the agency of *idem in alio*. The *idem*, the same impression, is to be restored, but *in alio*, in a different material—by means of some different instrument."

And again :

" If a man, taking a hint from the Roman *saltatio* (*saltavit Andromachen*), should say that he would ' whistle Waterloo,'—that is, by whistling connected with pantomime, would express the passion and the charges of Waterloo,—it would be monstrous to refuse him his postulate on the pretence that people did not whistle at Waterloo. . . . It is the very worst objection in the world to say that the strife of Waterloo did not reveal itself through whistling. Undoubtedly it did not ; but that is the very ground of the man's art. He will reproduce the fury and the movement as to the only point which concerns you, viz. the effect upon your own sympathies, through a language that seems without any relation to it : he will set before you that which *was* at Waterloo through that which was *not* at Waterloo— whereas any direct factual imitation, resting upon painted figures dressed up in regimentals, and worked by watchwork through the whole movements of the battle, would have been no art whatever in the sense of a Fine Art, but a base *mechanic* mimicry."

We are now led to a point at which a new aspect of the Imitation theory comes in. The word was not first applied to poetry by Aristotle ; on the contrary, it was much in Plato's mouth, and is one of the two supports which bear up his attack upon Poetry. For Plato, poet though he was, and lover of poets, could

yet find room for none in his ideal State;
and one-half of his case against them is
summed up in the word Imitation. You
will find the charge set out in the third
book of the *Republic*. Life, in Plato's
State, was divided into sections, like the
squares upon a chessboard; and justice,
the characteristic virtue of his community,
was to move on your own squares, and
never trespass upon your neighbour's.
But the poet is a trespasser.[18] He may
know little of leading an army, or steering
a ship, or mixing a posset; yet he pro-
fesses to be equally at home in all these
functions, and expects a hearing when he
speaks about them. Also, it is unworthy
of a man to be always speaking in the
person of others. Even Homer does it:
yes, he is the captain of the company of
tragedians, and, as often as not, speaks in
a part. Open the *Iliad*. For sixteen
lines Homer speaks, while he invokes the
Muses, and expounds the causes of the

D

Wrath.   But at the seventeenth it is no longer Homer but the priest Chryses who speaks.   Perhaps what he says and imprecates might be thrown into narrative form, and Plato gives a sample, and perhaps this might pass.   But then it would no longer be Homer!

The attack on Imitation is resumed in the tenth book from a different side, in connection with Plato's so-called " Ideas." The world, with the things which we see, is but a counterpart or imitation of the world and things which really are.   What then of the Painter and Poet?   The Painter copies what he thinks he sees in the world : not the things which are, nor even the things which seem to be, but his own notion of those appearances.   And so of the Poet.   So each is three degrees removed from truth and reality.

To this attack Aristotle does not refer. Yet in basing all Poetry upon Imitation, he takes up, surely with conscious purpose,

an impregnable position against it. Poetry
is, not accidentally but essentially, imitative ; it is so because of an instinct
which lies deep in our nature. Tragedy,
which is in the most obvious sense imitative, is also the highest branch of Poetry ;
and Homer is excellent because he knows
how to keep himself in the background,
and, after a word of prelude, introduces
a man or a woman—always one whose
character is distinct and individual. Yet
Aristotle allows for the possible abuse of
the mimetic impulse. The tragedian must
not overdo his part, or the charge of vul-
garity lies ; and a good play must stand
the test of being read at home, not depend-
ing for its success upon the incidents of
its public performance.

We pass on to the concluding words of
the Definition of Tragedy. Tragedy deals C. 6.
with the feelings of Pity and Fear, and
its operation is defined by the word

Katharsis, which we must now endeavour
to understand.   In the first place, I will
ask you to observe that Plato's case
against Poetry has another and a stronger
side than we have yet seen; and this is
precisely that which is concerned with
Pity and Fear.   Homer, or one of the
tragedians, exhibits a suffering hero, who
makes a long utterance about his woes, or
even weeps, or beats his breast; and the
spectator's heart goes out to such a sufferer.
Thus the emotional part of our nature,
which a strong man restrains within himself, and a wise lawgiver will wish to see
starved in others, is fed to satiety; our
sympathy is elicited in such a way that it
seems a virtue to give it; and that nobler
part of the soul, which should watch over
its mere impulses, is enfeebled and lulled
into a false security.   It will be seen that,
along with much that is whimsical, there
is a very solid groundwork here.   " Passive
impressions," says Butler, in well-known

words, " by being repeated, grow weaker " :
and so, in a sense, the more generous the
emotions upon which the tragic poet plays,
the more disastrous is the paralysis of moral
being which follows.   How does Aristotle
meet the difficulty?

First, just as we saw him doing with
Mimesis, he directly confronts Plato.
Tragedy, not by an incidental operation
which needs apology, but in its own
proper function, raises Pity and Fear.
Fear is defined [19] to be the pain or dis-
tress felt in view of a considerable evil,
nearly impending over oneself or some one
like oneself.   And Pity is much akin to
this ; only the person to be affected by
the evil must be, on the whole, undeserv-
ing of what befalls him.   Thus the death
or danger which in a play threatens the
hero, affects us, the spectators, with Pity
and Fear.   Now let us carry our thoughts
back to the poet of the early world—the
savage, as we called him.   He has an

impression of fear or pity fresh upon
him, and he wishes to reproduce it, and
to make clear to others what he felt.
Then he will go through in pantomime
some deed of horror, probably a murder ;
gesticulating and droning a wild dirge ;
and a thrill of horror or sympathy will
pass through his hearers. Thus he has, in
the strictest sense of the word, imitated
those elementary feelings—in this case,
those of Pity and Fear — which had
moved him. The Arts unfold themselves.
Tragedy, with all its appliances,—stage,
actors, musicians,—does in effect just what
the savage did ; it copies a deed of horror,
and communicates to the poet's audience
the thrill which the poet first felt in himself. Music, in its developed power, does
the same ; it reproduces, or imitates, the
same elementary feeling. Only Music
deals with a more varied field of emotions,
and does not confine itself to Pity and
Fear. Tragedy deals only, or mainly,

with those feelings : this is possibly to narrow its scope too much ; for other feelings—Admiration, for example, or Hope—are legitimate motives for serious drama. But in the conventional and historical[20] use of the word, which Aristotle accepts, suffering is essential. Tragedy then only exists in order to awaken Pity and Fear ; but how can it be held innocent in so doing ?

The answer lies in the word Katharsis. Tragedy effects a Katharsis of the feelings of Pity and Fear, or more strictly of the tendencies to those feelings, and it does so through Pity and Fear. No word of explanation is added in the *Poetics*. But in the *Politics*,[21] where the place of Music in education is under discussion, we find the key.

Certain kinds of Music, those namely which are exciting, should be listened to by the young rather than performed by them, since a passive attitude is necessary.

For all of us are susceptible, in different degrees, to the power of such Music. Watch a person of a specially susceptible temperament when the " sacred " melodies are played, and you will see him first excited, then calmed. The reason is that the nature was before overcharged with susceptibility : now the excitement has been called to the surface, and worked out of the system, which is left clearer and more healthy for its absence ; in fact, the man has been restored to his true and natural habit. And so it is with all according to the several degrees of their susceptibility to musical impressions. And so too with the tendency to any feeling, Pity and Fear being specially named : you may call up the feeling by an artificial process, and so get rid of it. Notice, first, that the metaphor is medical ; and, secondly, that the result is in all cases a *pleasurable* relief.[22]   " Such," says Aristotle, " is Katharsis in outline : hereafter I will deal with the subject more exactly in my treatise on Poetry." So far as the work in our hands goes, this promise is unredeemed ; but we can have no doubt what the main features of the explanation were. Only it seems right to assume that we should not have a mere repetition of the crude medical metaphor : it is essential, according to all Aristotle's teaching about Tragedy, that the purging should be effected by a tale of great passions and of a noble sufferer, that the feelings should be elevated as well as relieved.

Though the explanation of Katharsis in connection with the passage in the *Politics* is given with sufficient exactness in a note to Twining's edition,[23] yet much misconception has prevailed about it, and a vast amount of criticism, often valuable in itself, has been based upon erroneous views of Aristotle's meaning.[24] Indeed, I believe that I am correct in saying that the question has only been put upon a certain basis in recent times by Jacob Bernays.[25]   It is then remarkable to find that our own Milton, who was a diligent student of the *Poetics* and of its Italian commentators, has expressed so much of the true sense in his preface to *Samson Agonistes* :

" Tragedy, as it was anciently composed, hath been ever held the gravest, moralest, and most profitable of all other poems : therefore said by Aristotle to be of power, by raising pity and fear, or terrour, to purge the mind of those and such-like passions ; that is, to temper or reduce them to just measure with a kind of delight, stirred up by reading or seeing those passages well imitated. Nor is Nature herself wanting in her own efforts to make good his assertion : for so, in physick, things of melancholick hue and quality are used against melancholy, sour against sour, salt to remove salt humours."

Look again at the closing lines :

His servants he, with new acquist
Of true experience, from this great event
With peace and consolation hath dismissed,
And calm of mind, all passion spent.

If the words of the preface seemed to sketch out the merely physical view of the purgative power of Tragedy which we found in the *Politics*, these lines supply that requirement of greatness and nobility in the sufferings, which can never have been wanting in Milton's thought. But this side of the operation of Greek Tragedy is even more directly set out by a modern poet :

What hinders that we treat this tragic theme
As the Three taught when either woke some woe
—How Klutaimnestra hated, what the pride
Of Jokasté, why Medeia clove
Nature asunder—small rebuked by large,
We felt our puny hates refine to air,
Our prides as poor prevent the humbling hand,
Our petty passion purify its tide.[26]

We saw that Plato's case against Poetry rested upon two points—its imitative character, its appeal to feeling. We have

now seen that Aristotle, without naming
his master, yet probably in direct answer
to a challenge given in the *Republic*,[27] not
only admits the truth of the two allega-
tions, but makes them the foundation of
his own theory.   Poetry is in essence an
Imitation ; it works on and through Pity
and Fear, and purges those feelings.   Of
the sufficiency of the answer we are not
now called to judge.   But Plato, in his
later and more prosaic work on the *Laws*,
had returned to the attack.   When the
tragic and comic poets come forward and
ask for sufferance in the State, this is the
answer which they receive from the lawgiver : " Excellent sirs, we are ourselves
composers of a tragedy,— so far as in us
lies, the noblest and the best.   All our
state is framed to be an imitation of the
noblest and best life, and that is indeed,
as we hold, the truest tragedy." [28]   An
imitation of the noblest and best life.
The words seem, but only, I think, seem,

to supply something which is not in Aristotle, and to give a deeper and more noble conception of Tragedy than his. However this may be, the fact remains that Plato's last word to the poets is—— " Go." And Aristotle's word is of welcome. We will trust you, he says in effect, and we will trust human nature. Our citizens have wholesome human appetites, and if you were to offer them garbage they would not consent to feed upon it. Their digestion is vigorous, and man's common food will be good enough to nourish them. Here we notice Aristotle's faith in human nature, and also his generous desire to include in his scheme all which can enrich life and make it beautiful.[29] We see too his strong common sense, as he distinguishes between the thing and its abuse, and will not use the knife when only regulation is needed.

We have so far spoken at some length of the cardinal points in Aristotle's theory

of Tragedy ; and of Poetry, so far as it is
therein involved. Let us turn from his
speculation to his criticism, and observe
how he deals with actual Greek plays.
We will take the most concrete application of his principles ; and ask at once
which are his favourite tragedies, and
upon what grounds. The answer comes
quite clearly back. The *Œdipus Tyrannus* of Sophocles, and the *Iphigenia
in Tauris* of Euripides, are with him
standards of excellence, to which appeal
is constantly made. Both are plays of
high and manifold merit, the former, of
course, being the more famous. And
why are they selected ? Largely, but
not entirely, for the interest and ingenuity
of the plot. Take the *Iphigenia*. Instead of being really sacrificed at Aulis,
she has been rescued by Artemis, and
made her priestess in the land of the
Tauri, now the Crimea, where it is part
of the duties of her office to prepare, with

a certain ceremonial, all strangers for the
death to which a barbarous custom
doomed them. Hither comes Orestes in
the course of the wanderings appointed
by Apollo in expiation for a mother's
murder, and with him his faithful Pylades.
It is clear that a double recognition is C. 11.
now necessary; for neither does brother
know sister, nor sister brother; and this,
on one side at least, is managed with
extreme cleverness, and with much beauty C. 16.
of detail, and is highly praised by Aristotle. Again, this is a case where one C. 14.
person is about to do a dreadful thing
upon another in ignorance of their near-
ness in blood, and makes the discovery in
time to stay her hand; and this is the
most effective combination possible. And
further, the poet has shown good judgment C. 17.
in distinguishing between what came
within the story proper, and what was
to be introduced by way of episode. One
very curious feature in the play has not

Reversal of
fortune
& the idea
of relatives
taking leading part

been noticed by Aristotle, but illustrates more than one of his principles.   Orestes and his sister get down to their ship, and are making their escape (a messenger tells us) from the barbarous country, and the action might be thought to be complete. But a wind gets up,[30] his narrative goes on, which carries them back to shore, and they are again at the mercy of Thoas. Thus the knot is again tied ; and it is only loosed by the appearance of Athena, not otherwise a person in the play, *ex machina*, who announces that they are to go in safety, and that Thoas must not detain them.   Now why is this recom-plication introduced ?   Aristotle lays it down that the best plays end unhappily ; since when all leave the stage with friendly words, and a happy marriage is arranged, C. 13. the spirit of comedy comes in.   Now if the fugitives had simply escaped, snap-ping their fingers at Thoas, the ending would have been essentially comic : perhaps, after the grave and pathetic scenes which have gone before, we should rather call it burlesque. But the appearance of the *deus ex machina*, a device not itself to C. 15. be praised, enables the piece to be finished after all with dignity and elevation of feeling.

In the *Œdipus* most of the same merits are found. But Aristotle also, and specially, praises the skill with which the catastrophe is reserved ; it happens coincidently with the recognition of the hero's parentage, and so gains in power ; C. 10. and during a large part of the play the action is masked, so that every step which seems to bring Œdipus towards happiness and relief really leads him nearer to the abyss. Then the character is most happily chosen ; the greatness and generosity of Œdipus, taken with his obvious faults of obstinacy and self- C. 13. will, making him the ideal tragic hero. Aristotle censures a certain element of

E

absurdity in the plot, namely, where we are asked to believe that Œdipus had raised no questions about the death of his pre-decessor on the throne ; but this, as he says, lies not within the play, but among the antecedent circumstances, and there-fore is excused.

C. 15.
C. 24.

Another play which deeply interested Aristotle was the *Philoctetes* of Sophocles. It is hardly mentioned in the *Poetics* ; but in the *Ethics* [31] the author twice remarks upon the character of Neoptolemus, so generous that he could not abide by the lie to which Odysseus had schooled him, but gave in to the noble pleasure of tell-ing the truth. Now the *Philoctetes* of Sophocles is a play where the plot is highly ingenious, but is itself worked out of, and through, the characters, and mainly through that of Neoptolemus. It is therefore a play where plot and character are both conspicuous ; it was composed by Sophocles late in life, and

when he had before him a play by Euripides on the same story, as well as one
by Æschylus.

The *Choephoræ* of Æschylus is also
mentioned, with praise, in respect of the
particular form of Recognition which it C. 16.
illustrates. From the great beauty of the
recognition - scene in this play, and the
offence which some of its details ap-
parently gave, we could wish that the
critic's judgment had been more fully
expressed, and, it must be added, less
ambiguous.[32]

From the selection of these plays, Aristotle's leading principle in dramatic criticism is now apparent. It is the supreme
importance of Plot. This is pointed out
by a great English writer, lately taken
from us. In an early essay on " Poetry,
with reference to Aristotle's *Poetics*," Cardinal Newman writes :—

" Aristotle considers the excellence of a
tragedy to depend upon its plot — and

since a tragedy, as such, is obviously the exhibition of an action, no one can deny his statement to be abstractedly true. Accordingly, he directs his principal attention to the economy of the fable; determines its range of subjects, delineates its proportions, traces its progress from a complication of incidents to their just and satisfactory settlement, investigates the means of making a train of events striking or affecting, and shows how the exhibition of character may be made subservient to the purpose of the action. His treatise is throughout interesting and valuable.   It is one thing, however, to form the *beau ideal* of a tragedy on scientific principles; another to point out the actual beauty of a particular school of dramatic composition.   The Greek tragedians are not generally felicitous in the construction of their plots.   Aristotle, then, rather tells us what Tragedy should be than what Greek Tragedy really was."

The writer proceeds to examine three plays of acknowledged excellence, one by each tragedian : the *Agamemnon*, the *Œdipus Tyrannus*, and the *Bacchæ* ; showing that the interest of the play does not in fact vary directly with the elaborateness of the plot, since in only one of the three can the plot be said to be elaborate at all. And he instances the *Œdipus Coloneus* as one of the two most beautiful plays of Sophocles, yet one in which the plot is not striking.

We must first admit that Aristotle fully and deliberately adopts the opinion imputed to him : Plot is brought into prominence in the opening words of the book, reasons are afterwards carefully stated for placing it first among the six constituent parts of Tragedy, and the discussion of the features of Plot is much more exhaustive than that bestowed upon any of the other parts. And in taking this view Aristotle is at one with him-

self, and his whole method coheres.
Poetry is, in its operation, an appeal to
the feelings ; therefore Tragedy, which
makes this appeal with most strength and
condensation, is higher than the other
kinds of poetry ; therefore plot, which
embodies the appeal in its most immediate
form, is higher than the other parts of
Tragedy. Let us, however, observe that
Aristotle does not really undervalue character so much as his words may seem
to convey. He condemns several plays
because the characters are faulty, judged
by his own rules. He does not name
any play for censure because it is weak in
plot. It is true that he condemns all
which are episodic ; that is, where
incidents are strung together without
necessary or probable connection. But
then it is just in such a play that the
characters, however admirable, are pre-
sented with least force and directness. Is
not the *Œdipus Coloneus* itself an illustra-

tion ; since in that play, so entirely re-
deemed by the grandeur and tenderness
of its closing scenes, the reader is some-
what distracted, often perhaps offended,
by the number of the persons, and the
unconnected way in which in the middle
part of the play they enter and leave the
stage ? And Aristotle, though preferring
the elaborate plot, where the successive
scenes involve, so to say, ascending and
descending powers of happiness and misery
in symmetrical sequence, yet finds room for
that which is simple, and which interests
us merely by the character or the
suffering. He tells us that Character is
to be introduced for the sake of Plot, in
order, that is, to colour and vivify Plot.
Yet it is hardly a paradox to say, on the
whole view, that he values Plot so highly
for the sake of Character, as being the
vehicle and mode of its presentment.

Is it possible that we are inclined to
feel dissatisfied with Aristotle's scheme as

narrow and unreal, partly because it may
seem to leave little room for the one
Greek play which we probably know best,
and feel to have more modern and abid-
ing interest than any other—the *Prometheus* of Æschylus?   But in truth the
Prometheus is not faulty in plot, for it
has no plot : it holds us from opening
to close with unquestioned charm ; yet no
advance is made in the action.   Indeed,
the *Prometheus* is an exceptional play,
and proves, that is, puts to the trial, more
than one of the accepted rules of drama.

Passing from plays to poets, we find a
C. 13. few important judgments in the *Poetics.*
Euripides is the "most tragic" of poets ;
that is, by not refusing to have recourse
to the most obvious appeals to feeling, he
practically best succeeds in working upon
pity and fear, as it is the office of Tragedy
to do.   But this is true with reservations ;
in his management of the Chorus he is
unfavourably contrasted with Sophocles ;

and the practice of introducing choral
odes which are unconnected with the
action—mere lyrical interludes—is con-
demned in Agathon, and, by implication, C. 18.
in Euripides. The saying of Sophocles
that "he drew men himself as they ought
to be, Euripides as they are" is quoted ; C. 25.
the context showing [33] that Sophocles
describes his own aim as ideal ; and
Aristotle appears to endorse the statement. Agathon is mentioned as having
attempted a novelty by writing a tragedy
with fanciful names, like a Comedy ;
this Aristotle neither praises nor blames, C. 9.
though he points out the advantage to
the tragedian of the old practice of writing
on an accepted mythological foundation.
Few later poets are named, one Theo- C. 11.
dectes, a contemporary and friend of Aris- C. 17.
totle, being perhaps the most interesting.

We have spoken thus far of Tragedy,
because it is the subject of far the largest

part of Aristotle's work ; and even now we must leave untouched his actual canons of the drama ; a wide and interesting field of inquiry, in which Aristotle is followed by such great critics as Corneille, as Dryden, above all, as Lessing. We must speak even more summarily of the other kinds of poetry. As to their definition, one half of it—that which tells us what each is—will be derived from the definition of Tragedy, by making the suitable variations in the clauses which limit, in each case, the imitation. Thus Comedy will be the imitation of a trivial or ludicrous C. 5. action (and Aristotle provides us with an excellent definition of the ludicrous), but will in other respects conform to the nature of Tragedy ; Epic will proceed by way of narrative, pure or mixed, and not through persons acting ; and so forth. But the definition will be incomplete unless we can make clear what the office or function of each kind is, as the office of

Tragedy was to purge certain feelings. Aristotle expressly mentions a special kind of pleasure as arising out of each kind of poetry, and never to be confounded with that arising out of other kinds. The pleasure of Comedy is realised when the piece ends with smiles, and the bitterest enemies walk out arm in arm. The C. 13. pleasure which the Epic poet effects he does not explain ; but Sir Philip Sidney will tell us :—

" And with a tale, forsooth, he cometh unto you, with a tale which holdeth children from play, and old men from the chimney corner, and pretending no more, doth intend the winning of the mind from wickedness to virtue."

And so of Lyric.

What does Aristotle contribute to our knowledge about Poetry as a whole ? He ventures on no formal definition. It is clear that Poetry is, on his view, an Imitation of a certain kind, producing a

certain pleasurable effect upon the feelings.   But how to fill in the epithets left
in blank ?   The most pressing question
is whether Metre shall or shall not be
made essential.   The requirement is
omitted in such a well-known definition
as that of Mill [34] : " Poetry is thought
tinged by feeling, and overheard " ; or in
Shelley's, " Poetry is the record of the
best and happiest moments of the happiest
and best minds " ; or in Bacon's, " His-
toriæ imitatio ad placitum conficta " ; it is
left ambiguous in Coleridge's, " the best
words in the best order." [35]   How does
Aristotle help us here ?   I should say
that his answer is clear : metre is not the
most essential characteristic of Poetry, yet
it would be a misuse of language to call
anything a poem which is not metrical in
form.   I am aware that, in a passage in
C. i. the first chapter of the *Poetics*, he has
been thought to say the reverse.   But I
believe that neither the words which he

uses, nor the instances which he quotes,
in any degree settle the point against the
view of his meaning given above,[36] and
this although such examples of poetical
prose as the Myth in the *Phædrus* and
parts of the first book of Herodotus were
under his eye. Conversely, indeed, it is
true that all which is metrical is not
poetry. You might put Herodotus into
metre, and the result would be history of
a sort, not poetry. The speculations of
Empedocles on the physical world remain
physics and nothing else, though in hexa-
meters. But elsewhere, Plato and Aristotle
invariably assume that only what is metrical is to be called poetry ; nay, that
metrical writing and poetry are, for the
common purposes of language, convertible
terms. " In metre, as a Poet," says Plato,[37]
" or without metre, as a layman." "A
good sentence," says Aristotle,[38] "should
have rhythm, but not metre ; if it have
metre, it will be a poem."

But though we have no definition of Poetry, yet both Plato and Aristotle lay down distinctions which will help us to clear our view. "Give me an example," says a speaker in Plato's *Banquet*[39] (of a word which has a general and also a restricted use). "Poetry," is the answer ; "which is a general name signifying every cause whereby anything proceeds from that which is not into that which is, so that the exercise of every inventive art is poetry, and all such artists poets. Yet they are not called poets, but distinguished by other names ; and one portion or species of poetry, that which has relation to music and rhythm, is divided from all others, and known by the name belonging to all. For this is alone properly called poetry, and those who exercise the art of this species of poetry, poets." "The poet," says Aristotle, is a "poet in respect of his imitation." "The poet should be a maker of myths, not a maker of metres." May I

The highest poetry is ~~the~~ the musical voice of the Divine — as such it cannot be defined.

add another distinction laid down by a modern writer? " Poetry," says Coleridge,[40] " is not the proper antithesis to prose, but to science. Poetry is opposed to science, and prose to metre." Somewhere among these three sayings has not the last word been spoken on the subject, or shall we ever be nearer to a formal definition?

Perhaps none of Aristotle's contributions to our general understanding of Poetry is more fruitful than his profound saying that " Poetry is more serious and more philosophical than History, because it deals with universal truth, not with that which lies in details." Here we must notice that the conception of history is somewhat a narrow one, as it is identified with annals or chronicles; and also that Poetry is not to be held really to work by any dull process of abstraction or generalisation, but by the quick insight which sees the permanent or typical truth underlying the casual and individual instance.

C. 9.

The substance of the remark is well given
by an old English writer (I believe un-
consciously) :—

"Truth, narrative, and past," says
Davenant,[41] "is the idol of historians, who
worship a dead thing ; and Truth opera-
tive, and by her effects continually alive,
is the mistress of Poets, who hath not her
existence in matter, but in reason."

Then we have an excellent account of
Metaphor, followed out in detail, with
examples from the poets, of metaphor both
simple and compound. Power of metaphor, he holds, is the surest mark of the
poet ; for it cannot be learnt or got from
without, and is, in fact, the ability to see
those finer shades of likeness which underlie
nature, and which Bacon calls " una eadem-
que naturæ vestigia aut signacula diversis
materiis et subjectis impressa." Poetry is
the province of the man of enthusiastic
temper, or the man of ready genius : the
former is readily fired, and soon touched to

fine issues; the latter penetrates those delicate degrees of likeness which others miss.

But, after all, it is in Aristotle's teaching about the imitative character of poetry, and its power of stirring the feelings, that we must look for the essential part of his theory. From what we have said above, it will be clear that what it is and what it does, the imitation and the feeling, are closely connected ; and also that when he says that Poetry is Imitation, Aristotle is asserting its power to set forth a special and an elevated kind of truth ; and is answering the objection, dating from before Plato's time [42] that it was nothing but a glorified falsehood. Let us verify the meaning of Imitation as applied to Epic. After allowing for the power which lies in mere eloquence and rhythm, and for the subtler charm of association, is it not still the simple elementary feelings upon which the epic poet plays, reproducing and imitating them ? Take the most

F

familiar instances from the Latin Epic, understanding the word in Aristotle's enlarged sense. Read the story of the fall of Troy, or of the deaths of Turnus and Camilla, for pity and for fear. Read the burst of feeling in the second *Georgic* for the passion of pride of country. Or take those single lines,[43] which have a power beyond their mere words to represent a whole mood of feeling ; the passion of pity in—

Sunt lacrimæ rerum, et mentem mortalia tangunt ; [44]

the passion of despair in—

Arma amens capio, nec sat rationis in armis ; [45]

the passion of panic and indignation which breathes beneath the " drums and tramplings " heard in—

Ad confligendum venientibus undique Poenis ;[46]

the passion of the strength which stands unaided—

Inconcussa tenens dubio vestigia mundo ; [47]

the passion of a great and generous
failure—

Quem si non tenuit, magnis tamen excidit
ausis.[48]

Every mood of passion, and not the
sterner ones only, do the poets call up and,
in Aristotle's sense, imitate ; and where
this imitation fails, however wise the
thought or eloquent its expression, I think
we shall find that we withhold or grudge
the name of poetry.   Many lines and
passages there will be, perhaps even in
the great poems, which will not bear the
test.   Aristotle allows for dull reaches of C. 24.
Epic verse, where elaborate diction may
properly make up for the absence of other
charm.   But on the whole view, and in
his general work, the poet will be found
to imitate feeling : he holds up the mirror
to Nature, but it is a magic mirror, one
which reflects the deep springs of action
as well as the action lying before our
eyes ; not only the world of phenomena

(if we may turn Plato's words against himself), but the phenomena as they appear to the eye of genius ; that is, the realities which genius apprehends and can alone interpret.

I cannot hope that I have made Aristotle's conception of Poetry stand out clearly and completely, for the subject is difficult and our review must be summary. But I have endeavoured to touch upon most of the salient points, and to show where his guiding hand has helped those who have come after him. I have freely used the words of modern writers, not for the sake of ornament only, but that we might feel how modern, rather how true for all time, much of our author's thought remains. And as I began by stating reasons which made it likely beforehand that the book would concern us all, as being the first effort of criticism, as coming from a mind so comprehensive and so acute, as based upon the brilliant poetical literature of Greece, so I will now appeal to authority, and ask you to hear Milton's estimate of the place and value of a study of the *Poetics.* You will find it in his treatise *On Education* :—

" When all these employments are well conquered, then will the choice Histories, Heroic Poems, and Attic Tragedies of stateliest and most regal argument, with all the famous Political Orations, offer themselves ; which, if they were not only read, but some of them got by memory and solemnly pronounced with right accent and grace, as might be taught, would endue them with the spirit of Demosthenes or Cicero, Euripides or Sophocles. And now, lastly, will be the time to read with them those organic arts which enable them to discourse and write perspicuously and elegantly, and according to the fittest style of lofty, mean, or lowly. Logic therefore, so much as is useful, is to be repressed

to this due place, with all her well-coucht
Heads or Topics, until it be time to open
her contracted palm into a graceful and
ornate rhetoric taught out of the rule
of Plato, Aristotle, Phalereus, Cicero,
Hermogenes, Longinus. To which Poetry
would be made subsequent, or indeed
rather precedent, as being less subtle and
fine, but more simple, sensuous, and
passionate. I mean not here the pro-
sody of a verse, which they could not
but have hit on before among the rudi-
ments of grammar, but that sublime Art
which in Aristotle's *Poetics*, in Horace,
and the Italian commentaries of Castelvetro, Tasso, Mazzoni, and others, teaches
what the laws are of a true Epic Poem,
what of a Dramatic, what of a Lyric,
what Decorum is, which is the grand
masterpiece to observe.

"This would make them soon perceive
what despicable creatures our common
Rimers and Play-writers be, and show

them what religious, what glorious and mag-
nificent use might be made of Poetry both
in divine and human things. From hence,
and not till now, will be the right season
of forming them to be able Writers and
Composers in every excellent matter, when
they shall be thus fraught with an universal
insight into things. Or whether they be
to speak in Parliament or Council, honour
and attention would be waiting on their
lips. Then would there also appear in
pulpits other visages, other gestures, and
stuff otherwise wrought than what we now
sit under ofttimes to as great a trial of
our patience as any other that they preach
unto us. These are the studies wherein
our noble and our gentle youths ought to
bestow their time in a disciplinary way
from twelve to one-and-twenty ; unless
they rely more upon their ancestors dead
than upon themselves living."

Such, and so highly praised, is the
edifice of poetical criticism which Aristotle

reared.   It is simple in its lines, and has suffered from the ravages, as well as from the accretions, of ages ; but the hand of the Master is unmistakeable.   If I may be bold to pursue the metaphor, I would liken this work, not to the lofty and intricate buildings of lands richly favoured by Nature, but to such a homely structure as you may see in latitudes more northerly than these, among the great Scandinavian forest tracts, where Aristotle's ancestors and our own, the learned tell us, once lived and multiplied as a single race.   The house owes nothing to the quarry, nothing to the mason, and but little to the plane or chisel of the carpenter.   But every one of the timbers has been proved by the wise old builder, and found fit for his use : when the parent tree grew in the forest, it had been fed by an iron soil, and trained by storms, and strengthened by sunshine. The open beams of the roof are beautiful, as well as strong ; for they are round and shapely in all their length, and, being richly coloured by air and by vital juices from within, can return the deep glow of the firelight. The tree was matured through the lifetime of generations of men, and the building may hold together as long, perhaps, as Time himself. Enter, if you have opportunity: the doorway is narrow, but noble guests assemble, and the entertainment satisfies ; the welcome prepared for all is unfailing ; *and here too there are gods.*

APPENDIX A

[1] *Title of the "Poetics."*—Aristotle himself refers
to the work as τὰ περὶ ποιητικῆς, sc. τέχνης. See
Politics, 8, 7 (1341 *b*. 39); *Rhetoric*, 1, 11 (1372ᵃ 2),
etc. This title precisely corresponds to that of
the *Rhetoric* (*Poet*. c. 19). As there was no
English word "Poetic," and the familiar Latin
title "Poetica" was ambiguous, English writers
early coined the word "Poetics," following the
analogy of "Ethics," "Politics," etc. A word
used by Milton (see above, p. 70) and by Bentley
is plainly classical.

[2] *Order of Aristotle's Works.*—The expression
in the text is purposely vague, because we have
little knowledge as to the order of composition of
the various works of Aristotle ; nor is it very
material, since the oral lectures on the various
subjects with which he dealt need not have
followed any such order. It is probable that
after writing the logical treatises and the first
two books of the *Rhetoric*, he passed to the
Ethics and *Politics*, that the *Poetics* and the

third book of the *Rhetoric* followed, and that
the physical works and the *Metaphysics* were
later.

See "Aristotle," by Sir Alexander Grant, in
Blackwood's series, and the article "Aristotle" in
the *Encyclopædia Britannica.*

[3] Aristotle was born in B.C. 384, and died in
322.   Sophocles and Euripides had died in 406,
and there are no later dates of much importance
to be noted in the history of Tragedy.   Aristophanes, who had outlived the Old Comedy, died
early in the fourth century; on the other hand,
Menander, the great name of the New Comedy,
was not born till 342.

[4] See "Christianity and the Latin Races," a
lecture by the late Dean of St. Paul's.

[5] The translations are in the main adapted from
that of Twining.

[6] περὶ ποιητῶν α′β′γ′, πραγματεῖαι τέχνης
ποιητικῆς α′β′, ἀπορήματα Ὁμηρικὰ σ′, περὶ
τραγῳδιῶν α′, διδασκαλίαι α′.—Diog. Laert. Bk. 5.

[7] The Definition of Tragedy will be more fully
understood if it is compared with other definitions
drawn by Aristotle, such as those of εὐδαιμονία
or ἀρετή in the *Ethics*, or this of πόλις, which is a
κοινωνία of a particular kind, existing for a particular purpose :—

ἡ δ᾽ ἐκ πλειόνων κωμῶν κοινωνία τέλειος πόλις
ἤδη, πάσης ἔχουσα πέρας τῆς αὐταρκείας ὡς ἔπος
εἰπεῖν, γινομένη μὲν οὖν τοῦ ζῆν ἕνεκεν, οὖσα δὲ
τοῦ εὖ ζῆν.—*Politics*, I, I (1252 *b*).

It is also interesting to compare Dryden's definition of a play, which ought to be—

"A just and lively image of human nature, representing its passions and humours, and the changes of fortune to which it is subject, for the delight and instruction of mankind."—*Essay of Dramatic Poesy.*

(This definition is put into the mouth of Lisideius (Sir Charles Sedley), but it was "well received" by the persons who are supposed to take part in the discussion, after some demur on the ground "that it was only *a genere et fine*," *i.e.* that it contained no *differentia*.)

8 See Horace, *A. P.* 113-127, 153-178, 309-322.

9 τῆς ὀρχήσεως δὲ ἄλλη μὲν Μουσῶν λέξιν μιμουμένων, τό τε μεγαλοπρεπὲς φυλάττοντες ἅμα καὶ ἐλεύθερον· ἄλλη δὲ εὐεξίας ἐλαφρότητός τε ἕνεκα καὶ κάλλους τῶν τοῦ σώματος αὐτοῦ μελῶν καὶ μερῶν.—Plato, *Laws*, 7, p. 795.

οὕτως ἦν τεχνίτης (ὁ Τελέστης), ὥστε ἐν τῷ ὀρχεῖσθαι τοὺς Ἑπτὰ ἐπὶ Θήβας, φανερὰ ποιεῖσθαι τὰ πράγματα δι' ὀρχήσεως.—Athenæus, 1, 39.

"I can deeply sympathise in imagination with the Greeks in this favourite part of their theatrical exhibitions, when I call to mind the pleasure I felt in beholding the combat of the Horatii and Curiatii most exquisitely danced in Italy to the music of Cimarosa."—Coleridge, *Lectures on Shakespeare*, etc., 2, 13.

10 This practice of illustrating Poetry from Painting, and *vice versa*, is habitual in all lan-

guages. Its limitations are laid down in Lessing's *Laocoön*. The following passages illustrate the general tendency :—

πλὴν ὁ Σιμωνίδης τὴν μὲν ζωγραφίαν ποίησιν σιωπῶσαν προσαγορεύει, τὴν δὲ ποίησιν ζωγραφίαν λαλοῦσαν.—Plutarch, *De Gloria Atheniensium*, c. 3.

" Milton wrote in bronze. I am sure Virgil polished off his *Georgics* in marble—sweet calm shapes ! exquisite harmonies of line ! As for the *Æneid*, that, sir, I consider to be so many bas-reliefs, mural ornaments, which affect me not much."—Thackeray, *The Newcomes*, c. 35.

" I replied, 'That he confounded the operations of the pencil and the pen : that the serene and silent art, as painting has been called by one of our first living poets, necessarily appealed to the eye, because it had not the organs for addressing the ear ; whereas poetry, or that species of composition which approached to it, lay under the necessity of doing absolutely the reverse, and addressed itself to the ear, for the purpose of exciting that interest which it could not attain through the medium of the eye.'

" Dick was not a whit staggered by my argument, which he contended was founded on misrepresentation.

" ' Description,' he said, ' was to the author of a romance exactly what drawing and tinting were to a painter, words were his colours, and, if properly employed, they could not fail to place the scene, which he wished to conjure up, as

effectually before the mind's eye as the tablet or
canvas presents it to the bodily organ.' "—Scott,
Introduction to the *Bride of Lammermoor.*

[11] συμβέβηκε δὲ τῶν αἰσθητῶν ἐν μὲν τοῖς
ἄλλοις μηθὲν ὑπάρχειν ὁμοίωμα τοῖς ἤθεσιν, οἷον
ἐν τοῖς ἁπτοῖς καὶ τοῖς γευστοῖς, ἀλλ' ἐν τοῖς
ὁρατοῖς ἠρέμα· σχήματα γάρ ἐστι τοιαῦτα, ἀλλ' ἐπὶ
μικρόν, καὶ πάντες τῆς τοιαύτης αἰσθήσεως κοινω-
νοῦσιν—ἔτι δὲ οὐκ ἔστι ταῦτα ὁμοιώματα τῶν
ἠθῶν, ἀλλὰ σημεῖα μᾶλλον τὰ γιγνόμενα σχήματα
καὶ χρώματα τῶν ἠθῶν . . . ἐν δὲ τοῖς μέλεσιν
αὐτοῖς ἐστι μιμήματα τῶν ἠθῶν, καὶ τοῦτ' ἐστὶ
φανερόν· εὐθὺς γὰρ ἡ τῶν ἁρμονιῶν διέστηκε φύσις
ὥστε ἀκούοντας ἄλλως διατίθεσθαι, κ.τ.λ.—
Politics, 8, 5 (1340ᵃ33).

[12] τοῖσιν δ' ἐν μέσσοισι πάις φόρμιγγι λιγείῃ
ἱμερόεν κιθάριζε, Λίνον δ' ὑπὸ καλὸν ἄειδε
λεπταλέῃ φωνῇ· τοὶ δὲ ῥήσσοντες ἁμαρτῇ
μολπῇ τ' ἰυγμῷ τε, ποσὶ σκαίροντες ἕποντο.

   Iliad, 18, 569-572.

Compare *Odyssey,* 8, 256, etc.

[13] τὸ μέλος ἐκ τριῶν ἐστὶ συγκείμενον, λόγου τε
καὶ ἁρμονίας καὶ ῥυθμοῦ.—*Republic,* 3, p. 398.

[14] This view as to the two physical causes is
taken in the version of Avicenna :—

" Causae genetrices carminis in humano ingenio
duae sunt.   Altera delectatio imitationis et usus
inde a pueris. . . . Altera causa natura insitus
homini amor compositionis aequabilis et num-
erorum ; quum metra harmoniis natura propinqua
essent, propensi in ea animi protulerunt."—

" Poetica Avicennæ," c. 3 in *Analecta Orientalia*,
edited by Professor Margoliouth, pp. 85, 86.

It is also taken by Vahlen (*Beiträge*, p. 11).

[15] πάντες ἄνθρωποι φύσει ὀρέγονται τοῦ εἰδέναι.
—Opening words of the *Metaphysics*.

[16] τὸ γὰρ μανθάνειν ῥᾳδίως ἡδὺ φύσει πᾶσίν ἐστι·
τὰ δὲ ὀνόματα σημαίνει τι·ὥστε ὅσα τῶν ὀνομάτων
ποιεῖ ἡμῖν μάθησιν ἥδιστα. . . . ἀναγκὴ δή, καὶ
λέξιν καὶ ἐνθυμήματα ταῦτα εἶναι ἀστεῖα, ὅσα
ποιεῖ ἡμῖν μάθησιν ταχεῖαν.—*Rhet.* 3, 10 (1410
b. 10).

[17] Shelley's *Defence of Poetry* was written in the
year 1821, being an answer to Peacock's *Four
Ages of Poetry*. It was not published till some
years after the author's death

[18] " ' But the knowledge of nature is only half the
task of a poet ; he must be acquainted likewise
with all the modes of life. His character requires
that he estimate the happiness and misery of every
condition ; observe the power of all the passions in
all their combinations, and trace the changes of
the human mind as they are modified by various
institutions and accidental influences of climate or
custom, from the sprightliness of infancy to the
despondence of decrepitude. He must divest himself of the prejudices of his age or country ; he
must consider right and wrong in their abstracted
and invariable state ; he must disregard present
laws and opinions, and rise to general and trans-
cendental truths, which will alway be the same ;
he must therefore content himself with the slow

progress of his name ; contemn the applause of his own time, and commit his claim to the justice of posterity. He must write as the interpreter of nature, and the legislator of mankind, and consider himself as presiding over the thoughts and manners of future generations ; as a being superior to time and place.

"'His labour is not yet at an end : he must know many languages and many sciences ; and that his style may be worthy of his thoughts, must, by incessant practice, familiarise to himself every delicacy of speech and grace of harmony.'

"Imlac now felt the enthusiastic fit, and was proceeding to aggrandise his own profession, when the prince cried out, 'Enough ! thou hast convinced me that no human being can ever be a poet.'"—Johnson, *Rasselas*, chaps. 10, 11.

[19] *Rhet.* 2, 5 (1382^a21).

[20] Φρυνίχου καὶ Αἰσχύλου τὴν τραγῳδίαν εἰς μύθους καὶ πάθη προαγόντων.—Plutarch, *Quæst. Symp.* 1, 5.

"Chaucer's Monk had the true Aristotelic idea of Tragedy :—

> *Tragedie* is to sayn a certain storie,
> As old bookes maken us memorie,
> Of *him that stood in gret prosperitee*
> And is *yfallen out of high degree*
> *In to miserie*, and *endeth wretchedly.*

But the Knight and the Host were among the θεαταὶ ΑΣΘΕΝΕΙΣ.

> Ho ! quod the knight, good sire, no more of this :
> That ye have said is right *ynough* ywis,

G

> And mochel more ; for litel hevinesse
> Is right enough to mochel folk, I gesse.
> I say for me, it is a gret disese [uneasiness]
> Wher as men have ben in gret welth and ese,
> To heren of hir soden fall, alas !
> And the contrary is joye and gret solas,
> As whan a man hath ben in powre estat,
> And climbeth, and wexeth fortunat,
> And ther abideth in prosperitee :
> *Swiche* thin is gladsom, as it thinketh me,
> And of swiche thing were goodly for to telle."

From Twining's note 100. (The italics, etc., are his.)

[21] *Politics*, 8, 7 (1341^{b}39).

[22] καὶ πᾶσι γίγνεσθαί τινα κάθαρσιν καὶ κουφίζεσθαι μεθ' ἡδονῆς· ὁμοίως δὲ καὶ τὰ μέλη τὰ καθαρτικὰ παρέχει χαρὰν ἀβλαβῆ τοῖς ἀνθρώποις. —*Politics*, l.c.

[23] Twining, note 45. He quotes and carefully examines the passage of the *Politics*, remarking that the Abbé Batteux is the only commentator known to himself who had paid a proper attention to this passage. The note is unfortunately too long to be given here, and cannot fairly be represented by an extract. He does not in this passage, though he does elsewhere, mention the excellent Commentary of Robortelli (published in 1547), the importance of which was pointed out to me by Professor Veitch. Robortelli refers to the passage of the *Politics*, in speaking of the κάθαρσις effected by Tragedy ; but he goes on to explain the term of a certain training and direction of the feelings of pity and fear, and of a fortitude shown under

actual misfortunes, when those who suffer have
been accustomed to see that worse things have
befallen others. He quotes from the Comic poet
Timocles the lines (found in Athenæus, Bk. 5) :—

ὦ τᾶν, ἄκουσον εἴ τί σοι μέλλω λέγειν.
ἄνθρωπός ἐστι ζῷον ἐπίπονον φύσει,
καὶ πολλὰ λυπήρ᾽ ὁ βίος ἐν ἑαυτῷ φέρει.
παραψυχὰς οὖν φροντίδων ἀνεύρατο
ταύτας· ὁ γὰρ νοῦς τῶν ἰδίων λήθην λαβὼν
πρὸς ἀλλοτρίῳ τε ψυχαγωγηθεὶς πάθει,
μεθ᾽ ἡδονῆς ἀπῆλθε παιδευθεὶς ἅμα.
τοὺς γὰρ τραγῳδοὺς πρῶτον, εἰ βούλει, σκόπει,
ὡς ὠφελοῦσι πάντας. ὁ μὲν ὢν γὰρ πένης
πτωχότερον αὑτοῦ καταμαθὼν τὸν Τήλεφον
γενόμενον ἤδη τὴν πενίαν ῥᾷον φέρει.
ὁ νοσῶν τι μανικὸν Ἀλκμέων᾽ ἐσκέψατο.
ὀφθαλμιᾷ τις, εἰσὶ Φινεῖδαι τυφλοί.
τέθνηκέ τῳ παῖς, ἡ Νιόβη κεκούφικεν.
χωλός τίς ἐστι, τὸν Φιλοκτήτην ὅρα.
γέρων τις ἀτυχεῖ, κατέμαθεν τὸν Οἰνέα.
ἅπαντα γὰρ τὰ μείζον᾽ ἢ πέπονθέ τις
ἀτυχήματ᾽ ἄλλοις γεγονότ᾽ ἐννοούμενος
τὰς αὑτὸς αὑτοῦ συμφορὰς ἧττον στένει.

(See Professor Mahaffy's *History of Greek
Literature*, 13, p. 405, note 1.)

The thought recurs in the *Thoughts* of Marcus
Aurelius :

"At first tragedies were brought on the stage as
means of reminding men of the things which
happen to them, and that it is according to nature
for things to happen so, and that, if you are

delighted with what is shown on the stage, you should not be troubled with that which takes place on the larger stage. For you see that these things must be acomplished thus, and that even they bear them who cry out ' O Cithaeron ! ' "—11, 6, Long's translation.

[24] Thus Dr. Johnson, while touching upon Aristotle's point in his own vigorous explanation, goes on to assume that *all* the passions, and not pity and fear only, are to be purified by *admixture with* pity and fear.

" I introduced Aristotle's doctrine, in his *Art of Poetry*, of κάθαρσις τῶν παθημάτων, the purging of the passions as the purpose of tragedy. ' But how are the passions to be purged by terror and pity ? ' said I, with an assumed air of ignorance. . . . JOHNSON, ' Why, Sir, you are to consider what is the meaning of purging in the original sense. It is to expel impurities from the human body. The mind is subject to the same imperfection. The passions are the great movers of human actions ; but they are mixed with such impurities, that it is necessary they should be purged or refined by means of terror and pity. For instance, ambition is a noble passion, but by seeing upon the stage, that a man who is so excessively ambitious as to raise himself by injustice is punished, we are terrified at the fatal consequences of such a passion. In the same manner a certain degree of resentment is necessary ; but if we see that a man carries it too far, we pity the object of it, and are taught to moderate that passion."—Boswell's *Life*, ann. 1776.

Lessing (*Dramaturgie*, No. 48) explains the purgation of pity and fear to mean the reduction of the extreme of either feeling, whether in excess or in defect, to the mean. He found a "but" (ἀλλά) in his text, introducing the last clause of the definition, and is at pains to explain this by a special antithesis between narrative and dramatic poetry, the latter alone being sufficiently vivid to affect the passion in the desired manner. ·

Goethe (*Nachlese zu Aristoteles Poetik*, 1826) refuses to allow any *moral* import to the term κάθαρσις, which he explains of the compensation made, in a tragedy regarded as a work of art, by the hero's sufferings at its close. Referring to the passage of the *Politics*, he understands two kinds of music to be there intended, one which excites, another which tranquillises.

[25] *Grundzüge der verlorenen Abhandlung des Aristoteles über Wirkung der Tragödie*, 1857. (See Appendix B.)

Bernays did not discover the bearing of the *Politics* passage upon the κάθαρσις of Tragedy; for, as has been shown, this was understood by Robortelli in the sixteenth century, and also by the Abbé Batteux and by Twining. Bernays points out that the passage was known to Lessing and to Goethe, though turned to little account by either. Of the intrinsic value of Goethe's remarks he makes fitting recognition. He men-

tions with satisfaction Milton's appreciation of
Aristotle's meaning, and excuses the poet's rendering of κάθαρσις by "lustratio," as being
probably the work of a secretary. The main
points in Bernays' view, as contained in his paper
of 1857 and his letter to L. Spengel of 1859, may
be thus summarised :—

(1) κάθαρσις, in its æsthetic use, is a term
coined by Aristotle, and bears a specific sense.

(2) The key to this sense is to be sought chiefly
in the passage of the *Politics*, where the κάθαρσις
effected by certain kinds of music is defined.

(3) The object of Aristotle in that passage is
not *moral* improvement ; for he expressly finds
room for the lower kinds of music which Plato
rejects.

(4) The specific meaning which he intended
for κάθαρσις is (not sacrificial or expiatory, but)
medical or pathological.

(5) The *patients* are men, not feelings : πάθημα
being the condition of the παθητικός, the person
who has a tendency towards any πάθος. (It is
not certain that this distinction between πάθη and
παθήματα can be maintained.)

(6) τοιούτων, in the Definition of Tragedy,
means τοιούτων, not τούτων καὶ τοιούτων.

(7) Later Greek literature, and especially the
works of the Neoplatonists, shows that κάθαρσις,
as an Aristotelian term, was accepted in the pathological sense.

Not the least interesting feature in Bernays'

study is his confidence that the complete *Poetics* will some day be restored to us. When that day comes, we may be sure that Aristotle's doctrine will be approved as no mere phrase, but a well-reasoned and responsible judgment; and only less sure that the correctness of Bernays' reading of it will be established.

[26] R. Browning, *Aristophanes' Apology*, p. 10.

[27] οὐκοῦν δικαία ἐστὶν οὕτω κατιέναι, ἀπολογησαμένη ἢ ἐν μέλει ἤ τινι ἄλλῳ μέτρῳ; πάνυ μὲν οὖν. δοῖμεν δέ γέ που ἂν καὶ τοῖς προστάταις αὐτῆς, ὅσοι μὴ ποιητικοί, φιλοποιηταὶ δέ, ἄνευ μέτρου λόγον ὑπὲρ αὐτῆς εἰπεῖν, ὡς οὐ μόνον ἡδεῖα ἀλλὰ καὶ ὠφελίμη πρὸς τὰς πολιτείας καὶ τὸν βίον τὸν ἀνθρώπινόν ἐστι· καὶ εὐμενῶς ἀκουσόμεθα.—*Rep.* 10, p. 608.

This reference I owe to the kindness of Professor Murray, who pointed out the direct relevancy of the passage. The earnestness of Plato's language cannot be mistaken; and Aristotle's answer is conceived under an equal sense of responsibility.

[28] ὦ ἄριστοι τῶν ξένων, ἡμεῖς ἔσμεν τραγῳδίας αὐτοὶ ποιηταὶ κατὰ δύναμιν ὅτι καλλίστης ἅμα καὶ ἀρίστης· πᾶσα οὖν ἡμῖν ἡ πολιτεία ξυνέστηκε μίμησις τοῦ καλλίστου καὶ ἀρίστου βίου, ὃ δή φαμεν ἡμεῖς γε ὄντως εἶναι τραγῳδίαν τὴν ἀληθεστάτην.—*Laws*, 7, p. 816.

[29] "Aristotle desires to give music, as he also desires to give tragedy, and even comedy, its full natural verge and scope. He is more careful than Plato had been not to impoverish the life of

his State, or to curtail its opportunities of making a rational use of leisure ; he wishes its enjoyment of the goods of civilised existence to be full and complete."—W. L. Newman's *Politics*, vol. 1, p. 369.

[30] *Iphigenia in Tauris*, l. 1394 *sq.*

[31] *Ethics*, 8, 3 and 10 (1146^a19 and 1151^b18).

[32] *The Recognition-Scene in the "Choephorœ" of Æschylus.*—In classifying the various kinds of recognition, Aristotle assigns the first place to plays where the recognition is brought about in the natural unfolding of the incidents ; as Œdipus is made known in the *Œdipus Tyrannus*, or Iphigenia in the *Iphigenia in Tauris* ; the second to those where a " process of inference " is introduced. Of the latter sort he gives two instances. One is a play on the Iphigenia story by an author otherwise almost unknown : here the process was exhibited as taking place in the mind of Orestes, who reasoned thus :

My sister was sacrificed in Aulis.
Such things run in families :
Therefore it is natural that I should be sacrificed also.

This was overheard and he was recognised.

The other case is that in the *Choephorœ*, where Electra recognises her brother by inference. The two cases are not identical, since in the latter it is the person who recognises another, in the former the object of the recognition, who so reasons. But it is with the " syllogism " of Electra itself

that we are concerned. According to Aristotle
Electra argues thus :

> Some one *like* has come.
> No one is *like* except Orestes :
> Therefore Orestes has come.

All interpreters agree to complete the premisses
thus :

> Some one *like me* has come.
> No one is *like me* except Orestes.

If Aristotle really meant this (which is possible
on the words), he is imputing to Electra, that is,
to Æschylus, a fatuity which is not only not intended
by the poet, but which none of those who criti-
cised the details of the scene had found there.
The passage in Æschylus is 165-182. I quote
the analysis given in Conington's edition, itali-
cising some lines for convenience :—

" *Electra.* Now that the libation is over I see
    something new.

Chorus. What is it ?   How I tremble !

El. A lock of hair on the tomb.

Chor. Whose ?

El. One may easily guess.

Chor. Tell me.

El. There is no one here but me who would think
    of honouring my father.

Chor. No ; for his other kinsmen are his enemies.

El. The lock itself resembles——

Chor. Whose hair ?

El. My own.

Chor. Can it then come from Orestes ?
El. The hair is most like his."
The reasoning is surely clear :—

> Here is a lock of hair put in honour of my father.
> No one would have put it but Orestes :
> Therefore Orestes has come.

But Electra does not choose to name Orestes, and so expose her feminine readiness to believe what she hopes, and find reasons for what she believes ; and in fact she makes the chorus name him. She parries their point-blank question by saying, " I am the only person to make such an offering," and, " Why, the hair is just like mine !." but her own train of thought is never interrupted, and when Orestes has been once named, she lets out the conclusion at which she has long arrived : " The hair is most like his."

The reasoning is continued at 183. " I too am all perturbed, and know not what to think. *The offering cannot have come from any Argive— still less from my mother.— Yet how to fix it on Orestes ?* Oh, that it could speak and tell us ! May the gods look on our troubles ! they can aid us even now. See, here are footprints, just the size of mine—more and more anguish and per- plexity."

The argument from the footprints is of course a sophism ; but it is the sophism of a loving and despairing sister, and when it is uttered the speaker breaks down under her feelings. What could possibly be more true to nature ? Now

Orestes comes forward and tells his sister that her prayers are at last answered, and that he is before her. By a natural reaction of feeling she refuses to believe. Then gravely and gently he rallies her on this incredulity. " Now when I stand before thee thou doubtest, though the colour of my hair and the measure of my footprints seemed proof enough to thee a moment since. *See the place from which the hair was cut.*" In other words, " Your original thought—call it intuition or inference—was right. It *was* Orestes' hair."

This credulity, dear to a woman's mind, is often marked by Æschylus : see *Agam.* 264-316, 483, 484 ; *Prom.* 509, 510.

Now in this scene it would seem easy for an Athenian audience, so easily offended by anything irrational or melodramatic, to find fault with the identification of the lock of hair or of the footprints. But only malice or the exaggerated spirit of burlesque could so confuse the subsidiary proofs with the main reasoning as to make Electra say :

> Some one with hair and feet like mine has come.
> There is no such person but Orestes :
> Therefore Orestes has come.

And in fact Euripides, who has travestied the details of the scene, has not made this mistake.

In his *Electra* (l. 502) the old servant comes in excitedly. He has seen a sacrificed sheep on Agamemnon's tomb and a lock of yellow hair. " And I wondered," he says, " what man was he

who dared come to the tomb ; for it was certainly
no Argive : nay, but perhaps your brother is come
secretly." Here the reasoning suggested is :

> Some one has had the courage and piety to place this
>   offering on the tomb.
> No one but Orestes would do this :
> Therefore Orestes has come.

He goes on to suggest the tests of the hair, and
the footprints, and the garment ; absurd enough
when stated in cold blood, and rightly rejected by
Electra. Finally the recognition is effected in
the orthodox way, by a scar, a σημεῖον used
πίστεως ἕνεκα, which, if serious criticism were in
place, would, on Aristotle's principles, be con-
demned as frigid.

Let us turn to the *Electra* of Sophocles.
Sophocles is aware of the criticism which the
scene in Æschylus had provided, and is to show
his skill in avoiding it. Accordingly the argument
is put into the mouth of Chrysothemis, the less
heroic sister. She enters full of news. "Orestes
is come," she says. "Orestes is dead," answers
Electra ; "but give your proof." "I saw offerings on the tomb," says Chrysothemis, "and a
lock of hair, which I am sure was Orestes'. *For
no one else would have placed one there, I know* ;
not you, not our mother—so it was Orestes." "I
am really sorry," says Electra, "that you are so
foolish. Orestes is dead, and (in answer to a
question) these offerings were perhaps put there

in mourning for him.   So leave these imaginings and be practical."

Here again we have the reasoning :

> Some one like Orestes has come.
> No one is like him but himself :
> Therefore Orestes has come.

But it is entrusted to the weaker sister, and rejected by the stronger.

Aristophanes, in the *Clouds* (l. 531), says that his play has come to look for its sister-comedy, " for 'twill know its brother's lock if it see it," *i.e.* it will be as ready with its intuitive recognition as was Electra in Æschylus—" *The hair is most like his.*"

Can there be any reason for not supposing that Aristotle meant what Æschylus meant, and what Sophocles, Euripides, and Aristophanes understood him to mean ?—

> Some one *like Orestes* has come.
> No one is like him but Orestes :
> Therefore Orestes has come.

With regard to the particular fault which the audience, echoed by Euripides, found in the appeal to the hair and the footprints, there is something to be said.   It was clearly a mistake— one of the same kind as that noticed by Aristotle in the *Amphiaraus* of Carcinus—to put these details before so quick-witted an audience ; and if the play had to be acted again to the same audience, it would be wise to omit them.   And a dramatic

author should not write what cannot be acted.
But Æschylus knew that he did not in all things
satisfy his generation ; and in memorable words,
where bombast is out of the question, dedicated
his works "to Time." And surely to the reader—
who, says Aristotle again and again, has also his
verdict to pronounce—there is nothing in this
scene but the very truth of nature ; that delicacy
of character - drawing which the earliest poets
(*Poetics*, c. 6) best attained, before rhetoric and
elaboration of plot were made the supreme end.
It is to be remembered that this is not the only
case where Æschylus might have appealed from
contemporary critics. "The silence of Æschylus"
passed into a phrase ; that is, his habit of allowing
a Cassandra, an Atossa, a Prometheus, to be
exhibited in silence for some time, and only at last
to find words. Now this offended the audience,
but there were competent dissenters from its judgment : ἐγὼ δ' ἔχαιρον τῇ σιωπῇ καί με τοῦτ' ἔτερπεν
says Dionysus in Aristophanes (*Frogs*, 916).
And Longinus (c. 9), speaking of the eloquence of
silence, not with special reference to Æschylus,
may be taken to confirm the favourable judgment.

[33] πρὸς δὲ τούτοις ἐὰν ἐπιτιμᾶται ὅτι οὐκ ἀληθῆ,
ἀλλ' ἴσως δεῖ, οἷον καὶ Σοφοκλῆς ἔφη αὐτὸς μὲν
οἵους δεῖ ποιεῖν, Εὐριπίδην δὲ οἷοι εἰσί, ταύτῃ
λυτέον.

> "'Tis a speech
> That by a language of familiar lowness
> Enhances what of more heroic vein
> Is next to follow. But one fault it hath ;

It fits too close to life's realities,
In truth to Nature missing truth to Art ;
For Art commends not counterparts and copies,
But from our life a nobler life would shape,
Bodies celestial from terrestrial raise,
And teach us not jejunely what we are,
But what we may be, when the Parian block
Yields to the hand of Phidias."
                         Sir H. TAYLOR—*A Sicilian Summer.*

The view expressed in these lines is probably
that which Sophocles intended to convey ; it is
certainly that which Aristotle had in mind when
he recalled the anecdote ; as is clear from the
immediate context, and from the language which
he always holds about idealisation in character-
drawing (see, for example, c. 2 and c. 15). It is
thus tersely put by Dacier :—

" Sophocle tâchoit de rendre ses imitations par-
faites, en suivant toujours bien plus qu'une belle
nature etoit *capable* de faire, que ce qu'elle faisoit.
Au lieu qu'Euripide ne travailloit qu'à les rendre
semblables, en consultant davantage ce que cette
même nature faisoit, que ce qu'elle etoit *capable*
de faire." (Dacier's words form the text of an
admirable note by Twining.)

Bishop Hurd, in his Notes on the *Art of Poetry*
(of Horace), quotes these words of Aristotle (on
l. 317) and gives another interpretation. He
writes :—

" The meaning of which is, Sophocles, from his
more extended commerce with mankind, had enlarged and widened the narrow, partial conception,

arising from the contemplation of *particular* characters, into a complete comprehension of the *kind*.
Whereas the philosophic Euripides, having been
mostly conversant in the Academy, when he came
to look into life, keeping his eye too intent on
single, really existing personages, sunk the *kind*
in the *individual*; and so painted his characters
naturally indeed, and *truly*, with regard to the
objects in view, but sometimes without that
general and universally striking likeness, which is
demanded to the full exhibition of poetical truth."

He illustrates his meaning from the character
of Electra, who in Euripides carries her desire to
revenge herself upon her mother into unnatural
detail, while in Sophocles her expressions are
more general. In point of fact, Euripides is writing with Æschylus before him, and is following
Æschylus in bringing into prominence the murder
of Clytemnestra; whereas Sophocles, very possibly writing later than Euripides, made Ægisthus,
as in Homer, the chief criminal, the first object
of vengeance (see Jebb's *Electra* of Sophocles,
Introduction). Euripides shows up the weak
points in Æschylus; and his own treatment of the
character is narrow and "academic," very different
from that of the Electra in his *Orestes*.

Bishop Hurd's view is quoted by Lessing
(*Dramaturgie*, note 51) with emphatic approval,
on the ground that the high *moral* perfection suggested by that of Dacier is a matter of the individual, not of the type. Lessing's criticism is

contained in a note, and is avowedly not worked out.

After all, we must remember that we are dealing with an *anecdote*, perhaps fact, perhaps well invented, perhaps, as has, I think, been suggested, adapted from a passage in some comedy ; not with the weighed words of a philosopher.

[34] " Every truth which a human being can enunciáte, every thought, even every outward impression, which can enter into his consciousness, may become poetry when shown through any impassioned medium, when invested with the colouring of joy, or grief, or pity, or affection, or admiration, or reverence, or awe, or even hatred or terror : and, unless so coloured, nothing, be it as interesting as it may, is poetry. But both these definitions fail to discriminate between poetry and eloquence. Eloquence, as well as poetry, is thoughts coloured by the feelings. . . .

" Poetry and eloquence are both alike the expression or utterance of feeling. But, if we may be excused the antithesis, we should say that eloquence is *heard*, poetry is *over*heard. Eloquence supposes an audience ; the peculiarity of poetry appears to us to lie in the poet's utter unconsciousness of a listener."—Mill, *Dissertations and Discussions*, vol. i. pp. 70, 71.

[35] Coleridge's more formal definition should be recorded here :—

" Poetry is that species of composition which is opposed to works of science by proposing for its

immediate object pleasure, not truth ; and from all other species—having this object in common with it—it is discriminated by proposing to itself such delight from the *whole* as is compatible with a distinct gratification from each component *part*."
—*Biog. Lit.*

[36] Aristotle includes among works for which a place has to be found in a proper classification of the kinds of poetry, the Mimes of Sophron and Xenarchus, and "the Socratic Dialogues." If by the Socratic Dialogues is meant those written by Plato, Xenophon, Aristotle, *cadit quæstio.* But there is reason to think that he is referring to the dialogues written by a particular author ; which, in a fragment preserved from another work, are named in company with the Mimes of Sophron and Xenarchus, the point under discussion being precisely this, whether all those works are to be considered metrical or nonmetrical. The passage, the actual rendering of which is difficult, is as follows :—

Ἀριστοτέλης δὲ ἐν τῷ περὶ ποιητῶν οὕτως γράφει· οὐκοῦν οὐδὲ ἐμμέτρους τοὺς καλουμένους Σώφρονος καὶ Ξενάρχου μίμους μὴ φῶμεν εἶναι λόγους καὶ μιμήσεις, ἢ τοὺς Ἀλεξαμένου τοῦ Τηΐου, τοὺς πρώτους γραφέντας τῶν Σωκρατικῶν διαλόγων.—Athenæus (11, 505).

Now we do not know much as to the form of the Mimes of Sophron ; but we are told that a certain hymn of Gregory Nazianzene was composed after the models of Sophron, being not

metrical in the classical sense, but semimetrical.
The hymn begins—

> Παρθένε, νύμφη Χρίστου,
> δόξαζέ σου τὸν νύμφιον.

And the scholiast writes :

ἐν τούτῳ τῷ λόγῳ τὸν Συρακούσιον Σωφρόνα
μιμεῖται · οὗτος γὰρ μόνος ποιητῶν ῥυθμοῖς τισι
καὶ κώλοις ἐχρήσατο, ποιητικῆς ἀναλογίας κατα-
φρονήσας.

The inference would seem to be that all the
poems which Aristotle thinks might be left outside
altogether by a faulty classification resting on
distinctions of metre only, are metrical at least
in this limited sense.

The words in which this kind of poetry is
defined are these :

ἡ δὲ ἐποποιία μόνον τοῖς λόγοις ψιλοῖς ἢ τοῖς
μέτροις· καὶ τούτοις εἴτε μιγνῦσα μετ᾽ ἀλλήλων,
εἴθ᾽ ἑνὶ τινὶ γένει χρωμένη τῶν μέτρων τυγχάνουσα
τῶν νῦν.

Ueberweg has proposed to omit ἐποποιία, and
Bernays to introduce ἀνώνυμος before τυγχάνουσα.
The latter change has been approved by Vahlen,
who stated that the Oriental versions would be
found to support it. In point of fact, the Arabic
version gives support to both changes (see
Margoliouth's *Analecta Orientalia*, pp. 47, 48).
But if we introduce both, the general sense is
unaltered : only in place of a new and extended
class under the old name of ἐποποιία, we have a

new class hitherto unnamed. This class effects its imitation by language unaided (ψιλοῖς), *that is*, by metrical language. The word "unaided" seems to be fairly taken of the absence of aid from music : compare the use of ψιλομετρία in the next chapter, and Plato's ποίησιν ψιλὴν ἢ ἐν ᾠδῇ (*Phædrus*, p. 278) ; and the sense given to ἤ seems fair enough. Had Aristotle wished to express an alternative between prose and verse, he would surely have written τοῖς ψιλοῖς λόγοις ἢ τοῖς μέτροις (not τοῖς λόγοις ψιλοῖς).

This note is in the main reproduced from that of Tyrwhitt's edition. Metastasio (1782) speaks of the view taken here of the meaning being that of the majority of interpreters ; and he supports it against Dacier, who had wished to claim Aristotle's authority for a prose epic, by the opinion of Vettori, Castelvetro, and others. But among modern interpreters, Tyrwhitt seems to stand nearly alone, with MM. Egger and St. Hilaire. Metastasio himself seems to misrepresent part of Aristotle's argument (οὐδὲν γὰρ ἔχοιμεν κ.τ.λ.), as do the two French writers.

[37] *Phædrus*, 258 D.

[38] *Rhet.* 3, 8 (p. 1408[b]31).

[39] *Banquet*, p. 205 (Shelley's translation).

[40] *Lectures on Shakespeare*, etc. Wordsworth (in a note to the Appendix to his poems) also writes :—

"Much confusion has been introduced into criticism by the contradistinction of Poetry and Prose ; instead of the more philosophical one of

Poetry and Matter-of-fact, or Science. The only strict antithesis to Prose is Metre."

[41] Preface to *Gondibert*. So "Peindre sous l'homme momentané l'homme éternel" (Victor Hugo, *Quatre-vingt treize*).

[42] "Solon . . . went to see Thespis himself, as the ancient custom was, act; and after the play was done, he addressed him, and asked him if he was not ashamed to tell so many lies before such a number of people; and Thespis replying that it was no harm to say or do so in play, Solon vehemently struck his staff against the ground: "Ay," said he, "if we honour and commend such play as this, we shall find it some day in our business."—Plutarch's *Life of Solon* ("Dryden's" translation, ed. Clough).

Compare the saying of Gorgias :—

τὴν τραγῳδίαν εἶπεν ἀπάτην ἣν ὁ ἀπατήσας δικαιότερος τοῦ μὴ ἀπατήσαντος, καὶ ὁ ἀπατηθεὶς σοφώτερος τοῦ μὴ ἀπατηθέντος. — Plutarch, *De audiendis poetis*, p. 26.

[43] See Sellar's *Virgil*, end of chap. 11 (on the style of the *Æneid*).

[44] *Æn.* 1, 462.

[45] *Æn.* 2, 314.

[46] Lucr. 3, 845.

[47] Lucan, 2, 248.

[48] Ovid, *Metam.* 2, 328.

These passages and lines have been purposely selected from Latin poetry, as being slightly more modern, certainly more continuous with our own

literature, than the Greek, and therefore well suited
to an experimental and limited extension of Aristotle's principles.   To follow out the attempt into
the field of modern poetry would be beyond the
scope of these notes.   In the following extracts
from a Review of Lockhart's *Life of Scott*, by the
late Mr. Keble, a wider application is given to
principles identical with those of Aristotle on the
subject of poetical Imitation ; and the well-known
doctrines of the *Prælectiones* will be recognised
in English words.   I owe my own knowledge of
the paper to the kindness of the Rev. W. Lock.

" The idea, then, of poetry in the abstract is something like what follows : *Poetry is the indirect
expression in words, most appropriately in metrical
words, of some overpowering emotion, or ruling
taste, or feeling, the direct indulgence whereof is
somehow repressed. . . .*

"As far as these instances go, it would seem
that the analogical applications of the word Poetry
coincide well enough with Aristotle's notion of it,
as consisting chiefly in Imitation or Expression,
provided we understand that term with the two
following qualifications : 1. That the thing to be
imitated or expressed is some object of desire or
regret, or some other imaginative feeling, the
direct indulgence whereof is impeded.   2. That
the mode of imitation or expression is *indirect*,
the instruments of it being, for the most part,
associations more or less accidental.

" It would seem also that most of the leading

phenomena of poetry may be solved by this account of its nature. To take first that which is most obvious, its connection with metre and music. Setting aside all mysterious natural aptitude, such as universal experience appears to attest, in certain combinations and orders of sounds, as compared with certain passions and moods of mind in ourselves, the very task of metrical arrangement will fall in with the poetical instinct, such as has been above described, in two respects. On the one hand, it shapes out a sort of channel for wild and tumultuous feelings to vent themselves by; feelings whose very excess and violence would'seem to make the utterance of them almost impossible, for the throng of thoughts and words, crowding all at once to demand expression. On the other hand, the like rules may be no less useful in throwing a kind of veil over those strong or deep emotions which need relief, but cannot endure publicity. The very circumstance of their being expressed in verse draws off attention from the violence of the feelings themselves, and enables people to say things which they could not venture on in prose, much in the same way as the musical accompaniment gives meaning to the gestures of the dance, and hinders them from appearing to the bystanders merely fantastic. This effect of metre seems quite obvious as far as regards the sympathies of others. Emotions which in their unrestrained expression would appear too keen and outrageous to kindle fellow - feeling in any one, are mitigated, and become comparatively tolerable, not to say interesting to us, when we find them so far under control as to leave those who feel them at liberty to pay attention to measure and rhyme, and the other expedients of metrical composition.

"But over and above the effect on others, we apprehend that even in a writer's own mind there commonly exists a sort of instinctive delicacy, which finds its account in the work of arranging lines and syllables, and is content to utter, by their aid, what it would have shrunk from setting down in the language of conversation : the metrical form thus furnishing, at the same time, a vent for eager feelings, and a veil of reason to draw over them. All this, if it may be said without irreverence, would seem to be exemplified in perfection in the Psalms, and in those other portions of the inspired writings which take the form of impassioned poetry. From their perfect parallelism they are the most artificial of all compositions, yet none were so apt to relieve the deepest and most overflowing minds ; exhibiting therefore, by their very form, as compared with their matter, the perfection of that self-control which must itself be the perfection of a mixed creature such as man—'thoughts that breathe and words that burn,' exactly obeying a certain high law, and shaped by it into perfect order.

"This notion of the uses of metre as subsidiary to the end we attribute to poetry, may seem to be confirmed by reference to those compositions to which the term Poetry is applied without any sort of metre. Something will always be discoverable in them which answers the purpose just now assigned to numbers: of regulating, and thereby mitigating, the expression of feeling, and so reconciling to it both the writer and the reader. Thus, in the prose romances of Sir Walter Scott, and in all others which would be justly considered poetical, it will be found, we believe, that the story is in fact interposed, as a kind of transparent veil, between the listener and the narrator's real drift and feelings. The history of Waverley, or Henry Morton, or Ivanhoe, is but a pretext for the author's employing himself on those scenes, and characters, and sentiments which would best satisfy the cravings of his own ruling fancy. The rules of painting, sculpture, architecture, music, answer perhaps the same purpose, whenever we find in any of their provinces respectively what would be commonly denominated poetical composition. Men's attending to proportion, perspective, harmony, throughout the indulgence of emotions ever so vehement, is like articulation in the sounds they utter; it distinguishes our grief or joy from the mere sensations of infants or of irrational animals.

" Thus poetry, in its metrical form as well as in its substance, would seem to be deducible from two great instinctive necessities of our common nature—the same to which it was long ago referred by Aristotle : the need of some vent for absorbing or exciting thoughts which he calls imitation or expression; and the need of so controlling that expression, as that the presence of reason, subduing and ordering it, shall be felt, and make itself discernible throughout; which in this case becomes what he calls the instinct of harmony and rhythm."

See also Mr. Keble's Review of Copleston's *Prælectiones.* (Both papers are republished in Mr. Keble's *Occasional Papers and Reviews.*)

APPENDIX B

TEXT OF THE 'POETICS,' EDITIONS, &c.

THE *Poetics* was not included in the edition of
Aristotle which issued from the Aldine Press in
1495-98, but was first printed in Greek in 1508 in
the volume of *Rhetores Græci*. The Latin version,
by George Valla, had been published in 1498.
The text now accepted is based upon a single
11th century MS. Aᶜ (Paris, No. 1741), which
was used by Vettori (Victorius) in 1560, but the
palmary importance of which has been recognised
in modern times by Bekker and Ritter, and more
consistently followed by Susemihl, Ueberweg,
Vahlen, and others. The text, as settled by
Vahlen, is that now in general use. The labours
of Aristotelian scholars have done much to make
particular passages more readable ; though, from
the fragmentary condition of the treatise as we
have it, and the disarrangement which its parts
have probably suffered, the healing hand is comparatively helpless. Besides the names already

given, those of Spengel, Bernays, Bonitz—in still
later years, those of W. Christ and Bywater—may
properly be mentioned.

Much interest has attached to versions of the
Poetics in the Oriental languages preserved at
Paris and Florence ; since it has seemed reasonable to hope that the translators may have used a
fuller and better Greek text than any which has
reached us. The Arabic version (Paris, 882 A),
together with a fragment of the Syriac version
from which it was prepared, have now been
examined by the Laudian Professor of Arabic
(Professor Margoliouth) ; the results are given in
his *Analecta Orientalia,* which contains, besides the
Arabic text, a Latin rendering of the more signi-
ficant passages of the Arabic, and also a specimen
of the " Poetica " of Avicenna. While nothing is
contributed towards filling up the greater gaps in
the treatise, distinct evidence is given as to many
interesting points of reading. (See notes 14 and
36 in Appendix A.) The simplicity of the older
translator, his ignorance of Greek, and his verbal
faithfulness, are not without their humour. Thus
οἷον ἐν τῷ ᾿Αγάθωνος ῎Ανθει is represented by
" quemadmodum si quis unum esse bonum statuit "
(οἷον ἕν τὸ ἀγαθὸν ὃς ἂν θῇ) ; actors are hypo-
crites ; and the poet Carcinus becomes a common
crab !

A list of the more important editions and versions, and of works immediately based upon the
Poetics, is given in chronological order. It has

no claim to be complete, but will serve to show the number and variety of the workers in this field. It would be out of place to suggest any order of preference, otherwise than by saying that the majority of English readers may well be content with the works of Dr. Moore and Mr. Wharton, while those who only wish to read the treatise in English will find Twining's translation, reprinted in 1887 in Cassell's National Library, excellent : the text which he followed was too faulty to allow his work to be satisfactory to scholars. Twining's notes, which have not been reprinted very lately, are delightful reading from end to end. The great importance of Bernays' work has been indicated elsewhere.

LIST OF EDITIONS, &c.

VALLA (G.), Latin translation.   Venice, 1498.

Greek text among the " Rhetores Græci."
                              Venice, Aldus, 1508.

Latin translation, with the summary of Averroes.
                    Venice, Geo. Arrivabene, 1515.

PACCIUS (Pazzi), Latin translation.
                              Venice, Aldus, 1536.

ROBORTELLIUS (Fr.), " In librum de Arte Poetica explicationes."   Flor. 1548.

SEGNI (Bern.), Italian translation. Florence, 1549.

"Vinc. Madii et Barth. Lombardi in librum de Poetica communes explanationes : Madii vero in eundem librum propriæ annotationes."

Ven. 1550.

"Victorii (P.) Commentationes in primum librum Aristotelis de Arte Poetarum."

Flor. 1560.

Piccolomini (Alessandro), "Annotationi nel libro della Poetica d' Aristotele, con la traduttione del medesimo libro in lingua volgare."

Ven. 1575.

Castelvetro (Lodovico), "Poetica vulgarizzata e sposta."   Bale, 1576.

Heinsius recensuit.   Lugd. Batav. 1610.

Dacier, "La Poétique traduite en Français, avec des remarques critiques."

Paris and Amsterdam, 1692.

Goulstone (Theodore), Latin translation.

Cambridge, 1696.

Batteux, "Les quatre poétiques d'Aristote, d'Horace, de Vida, de Despreaux, avec les traductions et des remarques par l'Abbé Batteux."   Paris, 1771.

Metastasio (Pietro), "Estratto dell' Arte Poetica d' Aristotele e considerazioni su la medesima."

Paris, 1782.

TWINING (Thomas), "Aristotle's Treatise on Poetry, translated with notes on the translation and on the original, and two dissertations on poetical and musical imitation."

London, 1789.

[The Rev. Thomas Twining entered Sidney Sussex College, Cambridge, in 1755, and became a Fellow in 1760. His life was passed at Colchester: he had sole charge of the parish of Fordham from 1764, the year of his marriage, and latterly held the living of St. Mary's in Colchester till his death in 1804. See "Recreations and Studies of a Country Clergyman of the Eighteenth Century" (Murray, 1882) for a very pleasant account of his learned friendships, his driving tours in England and Wales, and his great dread of a French invasion, as recorded in his own letters.]

PYE (H. J.), "A Commentary illustrating the Poetic of Aristotle by examples taken chiefly from the modern poets. To which is prefixed a new and corrected edition of the translation of the Poetic." London, 1792.

MOOR (James, LL.D., Professor of Greek in the University of Glasgow), "On the end of Tragedy, according to Aristotle, an Essay in two parts." Glasgow, 1794.

TYRWHITT (Thomas), "De Poetica Liber. Textum

recensuit, versionem refinxit, et animadversioni-
bus illustravit Thomas Tyrwhitt." Oxon. 1794.

[This accomplished scholar was born in 1730,
and was a member of Queen's and Merton Colleges,
Oxford; he was an under-secretary of the War
Department, a clerk of the House of Commons,
and a Curator of the British Museum. The latter
years of his life were devoted to literature, English
as well as that of the ancient classics. He died
in 1786; his edition of the "Poetics" was a
posthumous work.]

HERMANN (Godfrey), Latin translation and Commentary.   Leipsic, 1802.

RITTER (Fr.), Latin translation and Commentary.
Cologne, 1839.

EGGER (M. E.), "Essai sur l'histoire de la
Critique chez les Grecs, suivi de la Poétique
d'Aristote et d'extraits de ses Problèmes, avec
traduction française et commentaire."
Paris, 1849.

BERNAYS (Jacob), "Grundzüge der verlorenen
Abhandlung des Aristoteles über Wirkung der
Tragödie."   Breslau, 1857.

SAINT-HILAIRE (J. Barthelemy), "Poétique traduite en français et accompagnée de notes
perpetuelles."   Paris, 1858.

STAHR (Adolf), "Aristoteles und die Wirkung
der Tragödie."   Berlin, 1859.

STAHR (Adolf), German translation, with Introduction and Notes. Stuttgart ——

SUSEMIHL (F.), German translation, with Introduction and Notes. Leipsic, 1865 and 1874.

VAHLEN (J.), "Beiträge zu Aristoteles' Poetik." Vienna, 1865.

VAHLEN (J.) recensuit. Berlin, 1867.

TEICHMÜLLER (Gustav), "Beiträge zur Erklärung der Poetik des Aristoteles." Halle, 1867.

UEBERWEG (F.), German translation, notes, and critical appendix. Berlin, 1869.

REINKENS (J. H.), "Aristoteles über Kunst, besonders über Tragödie." Vienna, 1870.

UEBERWEG (F.), "Ars Poetica ad fidem potissimum codicis antiquissimi A^c (Parisiensis, 1741)." Berlin, 1870.

VAHLEN (J.) iterum recensuit et adnotatione critica auxit. Berlin, 1874.

MOORE (Rev. Edward, B.D.), Vahlen's text with notes. Oxford, 1875.

CHRIST (W.) recensuit. Leipsic, 1878.

BERNAYS (Jacob), "Zwei Abhandlungen über Aristotelische Theorie des Drama" (the work of 1857, with other matter). Berlin, 1880.

I

BRAUNDSCHEID (F.), Text, German translation, critical notes, and Commentary.

Wiesbaden, 1882.

WHARTON (E. R), Vahlen's text, with English translation and notes. Oxford, 1883.

MARGOLIOUTH (D.), "Analecta Orientalia ad Poeticam Aristoteleam." London, 1887.

THE END

Printed by R. & R. CLARK, *Edinburgh*

MACMILLAN'S CLASSICAL TRANSLATIONS.

ARISTOTLE—THE POLITICS. By Rev. J. E. C. WELL-
DON, M.A. 10s. 6d.

THE RHETORIC. By the same. 7s. 6d.

THE ETHICS. By the same. [In preparation.

CICERO—SELECT LETTERS. Translated from Watson's
Edition. By Rev. G. E. Jeans, M.A. 10s. 6d.

ACADEMICS. Translated by J. S. REID, M.L. 5s. 6d.

HERODOTUS—THE HISTORY. By G. C. MACAULAY.
2 vols. 18s.

HOMER—ODYSSEY. By Professor S. H. BUTCHER, M.A.,
and A. LANG, M.A. 6s.

ILIAD. By A. LANG, M.A., WALTER LEAF, Litt.D., and ERNEST
MYERS. 12s. 6d.

THE ODYSSEY. BOOKS I.-XII. By the EARL OF CARNARVON.
8s. 6d.

HORACE. By J. LONSDALE, M.A., and S. LEE, M.A.
3s. 6d.

JUVENAL — THIRTEEN SATIRES. By A. LEEPER,
M.A. 3s. 6d.

LIVY. BOOKS XXI.-XXV. By Rev. A. J. CHURCH, M.A.,
and W. J. BRODRIBB, M.A. 7s. 6d.

PINDAR — ODES. By ERNEST MYERS, M.A. Second
Edition. 5s.

PLATO—REPUBLIC. By J. LL. DAVIES, M.A., and D. J.
VAUGHAN, M.A. 4s. 6d.

EUTHYPHRO, APOLOGY, CRITO, AND PHÆDO. By F. J.
CHURCH. 4s. 6d.

PHÆDRUS, LYSIS, AND PROTAGORAS. By Rev. J. WRIGHT,
M.A. 4s. 6d.

POLYBIUS—THE HISTORIES. By E. S. SHUCKBURGH.
2 vols. 24s.

SALLUST—CATILINE AND JUGURTHA. By A. W.
POLLARD, B.A. 6s. The Catiline, 3s.

TACITUS. By A. J. CHURCH, M.A., and W. J. BRODRIBB,
M.A. History, 6s. Annals, 7s. 6d. Agricola and Germania,
4s. 6d.

THEOCRITUS, BION, AND MOSCHUS. By A. LANG,
M.A. 4s. 6d.

VIRGIL. By J. LONSDALE, M.A., and S. LEE, M.A. 3s. 6d.

THE ÆNEID. By J. W. MACKAIL, M.A. 7s. 6d.

XENOPHON—COMPLETE WORKS. By H. G. DAKYNS,
M.A. With Introduction and Essays. 4 vols. Vol. I., containing
"The Anabasis" and "The Hellenica." 10s. 6d.

[Vol. II. in the Press.

MACMILLAN AND CO., LONDON.

MACMILLAN'S CLASSICAL LIBRARY.

ÆSCHYLUS—THE "SEVEN AGAINST THEBES." (With Translation.) By A. W. VERRALL, Litt.D. 8vo. 7s. 6d.

AGAMEMNON. Edited, with Introduction, Commentary, and Translation, by A. W. VERRALL, Litt.D. 8vo. 12s.

THE SUPPLICES. (With Translation.) By T. G. TUCKER, M.A. 8vo. 10s. 6d.

BABRIUS. By W. G. RUTHERFORD, M.A., LL.D. 12s. 6d.

CICERO—ACADEMICA. By J. S. REID, M.L. 15s.

EURIPIDES—MEDEA. By A. W. VERRALL, Litt.D. 7s. 6d.

HERODOTUS. BOOKS I.-III. By Professor A. H. SAYCE. 16s.

HOMER—ILIAD. 2 vols. Vol. I. Books I.-XII. Vol. II. Books XIII.-XXIV. By WALTER LEAF, Litt.D. 14s. each.

JUVENAL — THIRTEEN SATIRES. By Professor J. E. B. MAYOR. Vol. I. Fourth Edition. 10s. 6d. Vol. II. 10s. 6d.

KTESIAS — THE FRAGMENTS OF THE PERSIKA OF KTESIAS. Edited, with Introduction and Notes, by JOHN GILMORE, M.A. 8s. 6d.

PINDAR — NEMEAN ODES. By J. B. BURY, M.A. 12s.

PLATO — PHÆDO. By R. D. ARCHER-HIND, M.A. 8s. 6d.

TIMÆUS. By the same Editor. 8vo. 16s.

PLINY—LETTERS TO TRAJAN. Edited by E. G. HARDY, M.A. 10s. 6d.

TACITUS—ANNALS. By Professor G. O. HOLBROOKE, 16s.

THE HISTORIES. Edited, with Introduction and Notes, by Rev. W. A. SPOONER, M.A. 16s.

THUCYDIDES. BOOK IV. Revised Text, Illustrating the Principal Causes of Corruption in the Manuscripts of this Author. By W. G. RUTHERFORD, M.A. 7s. 6d.

MACMILLAN AND CO., LONDON.

MACMILLAN'S CLASSICAL SERIES.

Fcap. 8vo.   Cloth.

ÆSCHINES—IN CTESIPHONTA.   Edited by Rev. T. GWATKIN, M.A., and E. S. SHUCKBURGH, M.A.   5s.

ÆSCHYLUS—PERSÆ.   Edited by A. O. PRICKARD, M.A. With Map.   2s. 6d.

THE "SEVEN AGAINST THEBES."   Edited by A. W. VERRALL, Litt.D., and M. A. BAYFIELD, M.A.   2s. 6d.

ANDOCIDES — DE MYSTERIIS.   Edited by W. J. HICKIE, M.A.   2s. 6d.

ATTIC ORATORS, SELECTIONS FROM THE.   Antiphon, Andocides, Lysias, Isocrates, and Isæus.   Edited by R. C. JEBB, Litt.D.   5s.

CÆSAR—THE GALLIC WAR.   Edited after Kraner by Rev. J. BOND, M.A., and Rev. A. S. WALPOLE, M.A.   With Maps. 4s. 6d.

CATULLUS—SELECT POEMS.   Edited by F. P. SIMPSON, B.A.   3s. 6d.   [The Text of this Edition is carefully adapted to School use.]

CICERO—THE CATILINE ORATIONS.   From the German of Karl Halm.   Edited by A. S. WILKINS, Litt.D.   2s. 6d.

PRO LEGE MANILIA.   Edited, after Halm, by Professor A. S. WILKINS, Litt.D.   2s. 6d.

THE SECOND PHILIPPIC ORATION.   From the German of Karl Halm.   Edited, with Corrections and Additions, by Professor J. E. B. MAYOR.   3s. 6d.

PRO ROSCIO AMERINO.   Edited, after Halm, by E. H. DONKIN, M.A.   2s. 6d.

PRO P. SESTIO.   Edited by Rev. H. A. HOLDEN, M.A.   3s. 6d.

SELECT LETTERS.   Edited by Professor R. Y. TYRRELL, M.A.

DEMOSTHENES—DE CORONA.   Edited by B. DRAKE, M.A.   New and revised edition.   3s. 6d.

ADVERSUS LEPTINEM.   Edited by Rev. J. R. KING, M.A. 2s. 6d.

THE FIRST PHILIPPIC.   Edited, after C. Rehdantz, by Rev. T. GWATKIN.   2s. 6d.

EURIPIDES—HIPPOLYTUS.   Edited by Professor J. P. MAHAFFY and J. B. BURY.   2s. 6d.

MEDEA.   Edited by A. W. VERRALL, Litt.D.   2s. 6d.
IPHIGENIA IN TAURIS.   Edited by E. B. ENGLAND, M.A.   3s.
ION.   Edited by M. A. BAYFIELD, M.A.   2s. 6d.

MACMILLAN AND CO., LONDON.

MACMILLAN'S CLASSICAL SERIES.

Fcap. 8vo. Cloth.

HERODOTUS. BOOK III. Edited by G. C. MACAULAY, M.A. 2s. 6d.

BOOK VI. Edited by Professor J. STRACHAN, M.A. 3s. 6d.

BOOK VII. Edited by Mrs. MONTAGU BUTLER. 3s. 6d.

HOMER—ILIAD. BOOKS I., IX., XI., XVI.-XXIV. THE STORY OF ACHILLES. Edited by J. H. PRATT, M.A., and W. LEAF, Litt.D. 5s.

ODYSSEY. BOOK IX. Edited by Professor J. E. B. MAYOR, M.A. 2s. 6d.

ODYSSEY. BOOKS XXI.-XXIV. THE TRIUMPH OF ODYSSEUS. Edited by S. G. HAMILTON, B.A. 2s. 6d.

HORACE—THE ODES. Edited by T. E. PAGE, M.A. 5s. (Books I., II., III., and IV. separately, 2s. each).

THE SATIRES. Edited by Professor A. PALMER, M.A. 5s.

THE EPISTLES AND ARS POETICA. Edited by Professor A. S. WILKINS, Litt.D. 5s.

JUVENAL—THIRTEEN SATIRES. Edited, for the use of Schools, by E. G. HARDY, M.A. 5s. [The Text of this Edition is carefully adapted to School use.]

SELECT SATIRES. Edited by Professor JOHN E. B. MAYOR. X. and XI., 3s. 6d. XII.-XVI., 4s. 6d.

LIVY. BOOKS II. and III. Edited by Rev. H. M. STEPHENSON, M.A. 3s. 6d.

BOOKS XXI. and XXII. Edited by Rev. W. W. CAPES, M.A. 4s. 6d.

BOOKS XXIII. and XXIV. Edited by G. C. MACAULAY. With Maps. 3s. 6d.

THE LAST TWO KINGS OF MACEDON. Extracts from the Fourth and Fifth Decades of Livy. Selected and Edited by F. H. RAWLINS, M.A. With Maps. 2s. 6d.

LUCRETIUS. BOOKS I.-III. Edited by J. H. WARBURTON LEE, M.A. 3s. 6d.

LYSIAS—SELECT ORATIONS. Edited by E. S. SHUCKBURGH, M.A. 5s.

MARTIAL—SELECT EPIGRAMS. Edited by Rev. H. M. STEPHENSON, M.A. 5s.

OVID—FASTI. Edited by G. H. HALLAM, M.A. With Maps. 3s. 6d.

HEROIDUM EPISTULÆ XIII. Edited by E. S. SHUCKBURGH, M.A. 3s. 6d.

METAMORPHOSES. BOOKS XIII. and XIV. Edited by C. SIMMONS, M.A. 3s. 6d.

MACMILLAN AND CO., LONDON.

MACMILLAN'S CLASSICAL SERIES.

Fcap. 8vo. Cloth.

PLATO—THE REPUBLIC. BOOKS I.-V. Edited by
T. H. WARREN, M.A. 5s.

LACHES. Edited by M. T. TATHAM, M.A. 2s. 6d.

PLAUTUS—MILES GLORIOSUS. Edited by Professor R.
Y. TYRRELL, M.A. 3s. 6d.

AMPHITRUO. Edited by A. PALMER, M.A. 3s. 6d.

CAPTIVI. Edited by A. RHYS-SMITH, M.A.

PLINY—LETTERS. BOOKS I. and II. Edited by J.
COWAN, M.A. 3s.

LETTERS. BOOK III. Edited by Professor J. E. B.
MAYOR. With Life of Pliny by G. H. RENDALL. 3s. 6d.

PLUTARCH—LIFE OF THEMISTOKLES. Edited by
Rev. H. A. HOLDEN, M.A., LL.D. 3s. 6d.

LIVES OF GALBA AND OTHO. Edited by E. G.
HARDY, M.A. 5s.

POLYBIUS. The History of the Achæan League as contained in the remains of Polybius. Edited by W. W.
CAPES. 5s.

PROPERTIUS—SELECT POEMS. Edited by Professor
J. P. POSTGATE, M.A. 5s.

SALLUST—CATILINE AND JUGURTHA. Edited by
C. MERIVALE, D.D. 3s. 6d. Or separately, 2s. each.

BELLUM CATULINÆ. Edited by A. M. COOK, M.A.
2s. 6d.

TACITUS—AGRICOLA AND GERMANIA. Edited by
A. J. CHURCH, M.A., and W. J. BRODRIBB, M.A.
3s. 6d. Or separately, 2s. each.

THE ANNALS. BOOK VI. By the same Editors. 2s.

THE HISTORIES. BOOKS I. and II. Edited by A.
D. GODLEY, M.A. 3s. 6d.

THE HISTORIES. BOOKS III.-V. By the same
Editor. 3s. 6d.

TERENCE—HAUTON TIMORUMENOS. Edited by E.
S. SHUCKBURGH, M.A. 2s. 6d. With Translation.
3s. 6d.

PHORMIO. Edited by Rev. J. BOND, M.A., and Rev.
A. S. WALPOLE, M.A. 2s. 6d.

MACMILLAN AND CO., LONDON.

MACMILLAN'S CLASSICAL SERIES.

Fcap. 8vo.   Cloth.

THUCYDIDES. BOOK II.   Edited by E. C. MARCHANT, M.A.

BOOK IV.   Edited by C. E. GRAVES, M.A.   3s. 6d.

BOOK V.   By the same Editor.

BOOKS VI. and VII.   THE SICILIAN EXPEDITION. Edited by Rev. P. FROST, M.A.   With Map.   3s. 6d.

VIRGIL—ÆNEID. BOOKS II. and III.   THE NARRATIVE OF ÆNEAS.   Edited by E. W. HOWSON, M.A.   2s.

XENOPHON—HELLENICA. BOOKS I. and II.   Edited by H. HAILSTONE, M.A.   2s. 6d.

CYROPÆDIA.   BOOKS VII. and VIII.   Edited by Professor A. GOODWIN, M.A.   2s. 6d.

MEMORABILIA SOCRATIS.   Edited by A. R. CLUER, B.A.   5s.

THE ANABASIS.   BOOKS I.-IV.   Edited by Professors W. W. GOODWIN and J. W. WHITE.   Adapted to Goodwin's Greek Grammar.   With a Map.   3s. 6d.

HIERO.   Edited by Rev. H. A. HOLDEN, M.A., LL.D. 2s. 6d.

ŒCONOMICUS.   By the same Editor.   With Introduction, Explanatory Notes, Critical Appendix, and Lexicon. 5s.

The following are in preparation :—

DEMOSTHENES—IN MIDIAM.   Edited by Professor A. S. WILKINS, Litt.D., and HERMAN HAGER, Ph.D.

EURIPIDES — BACCHÆ.   Edited by Professor R. Y. TYRRELL, M.A.

HERODOTUS. BOOK V.   Edited by Professor J. STRACHAN, M.A.

ISÆOS—THE ORATIONS.   Edited by Professor WILLIAM RIDGEWAY, M.A.

OVID—METAMORPHOSES. BOOKS I.-III.   Edited by C. SIMMONS, M.A.

SALLUST—JUGURTHA.   Edited by A. M. COOK, M.A.

TACITUS—THE ANNALS. BOOKS I. and II.   Edited by J. S. REID, Litt.D.

Other Volumes will follow.

MACMILLAN AND CO., LONDON.